Thomas Webster

Life of Rev. James Richardson

A Bishop of the Methodist Episcopal Church in Canada

Thomas Webster

Life of Rev. James Richardson
A Bishop of the Methodist Episcopal Church in Canada

ISBN/EAN: 9783337161941

Printed in Europe, USA, Canada, Australia, Japan

Cover: Foto ©Lupo / pixelio.de

More available books at **www.hansebooks.com**

LIFE OF
REV. JAMES RICHARDSON,

A BISHOP OF THE

METHODIST EPISCOPAL CHURCH
IN CANADA,

BY THOMAS WEBSTER, D.D.,

Author of "History of M. E. Church in Canada," "Woman Man's Equal," etc.

WITH

INTRODUCTION

BY REV. BISHOP CARMAN, D.D.

"The fruit of the righteous is a tree of life: and he that winneth souls is wise."

TORONTO:

J. B. MAGURN, PUBLISHER,

36 KING STREET EAST.

1876.

Entered according to Act of Parliament of Canada, in the year one thousand eight hundred and seventy-six, by J. B. MAGURN, in the office of the Minister of Agriculture.

	PAGE
Introduction	i to xxviii
Birth—Parentage—	17
Enters the Service	38
His Marriage—Ret... —Called to preach	67
Enters the Itineran...	97
The Conference of...	119
Removal to State of... to Canada	156
Elected to the Episc...	179
Albert College—Jo...	192
General Conferenc... ordination of Bishop Carman—Las...	208
The Funeral—Me...	225

INTRODUCTION

TO DR. WEBSTER'S LIFE OF

BISHOP RICHARDSON;

BY

BISHOP CARMAN.

When one, that leaves any impress on society at all, has died, we know him better than while he was living. We view his actions and judge his motives with less bias: we set a fairer estimate upon his character; and with a calmer eye, in a clearer light, we perceive the ruling principles of his conduct and the results of his labors. If the will and the way have been evil, the general tendency of our nature —bad as it is sometimes said to be—is *not* to set down aught in malice, but to search out an excuse. And if they have been right, it is a pleasure to the mind to recall them, and a strength to virtue and a joy to the heart to hold them in remembrance.

Because these things are so, the review of the life of a good man can never cease to be both a benefit and a pleasure. Imperfections he may have; errors he may have committed; but the very grandeur of a man is to struggle above imperfections, and, in moral worth, to shine out beyond errors, so that his excellence is acknowledged, and his life on the earth beams with a perpetual lustre. The steady course of the upright man compels admiration. Kindness in the heart and purity in the life levy a tribute of respect and love on all the generations of men. Our moral instincts are the grandest safeguard of the race, and the hope of religion and truth; to them we must ever appeal. Since the human heart is what it is, and the incentives to virtue and to vice are what they are, human life is that one profound problem, that one solemn and tremendous conflict, from which not one of us stands aside a curious student or an uninterested spectator, but in whose issues our best possessions and our highest happiness are most deeply involved. Wherefore every man that casts the force of his convictions, the energy of his soul and the weight of his character on the side of the good and the true, while he serves his God in his generation, confers an inestimable blessing on his species. He demonstrates that, with all our weaknesses and disadvantages, a purer life is possible to all men; and to all that choose it, it is the safest pathway to honor and felicity.

In presenting the life and character of JAMES RICHARDSON to the public view, Dr. Webster is certainly furnishing such an encouragement and support to religion and virtue. And not only to virtue as taught in the schools, as exemplified and praised in heathen philosophy, but to religion as given in the Holy Scriptures,—the power of God that cometh down from Heaven and worketh wondrously in the hearts of men. To JAMES RICHARDSON religion was not merely a negative condition, a neutral ground; it was a positive, vigorous life. It was its province to assimilate all the elements of our manhood to its nature, and to mould the entire being. To him religion meant Christianity. It was not Naturalism, but Supernaturalism. It was not a decent Deism or an orderly Rationalism laying a sickly hand on the arm of man, the pilgrim and warrior, and speaking to him in a faint whisper of duty and destiny. It was an energy in the heart, co-operating with the Reason, and refining and directing the Affections; it was a force in society, forming the institutions, elevating the conceptions, inspiring the aims, and controlling the conduct of men. It laid a firm grasp upon evil, to check it and cast it out; it sustained and protected the right with an omnipotent arm; and it spake in plain words, with strong voice and unfaltering accents, of the relations and engagements of this life, and the prospects and claims of the life to come.

When a man with penetrating mind, extensive information and sound judgment gives in the adhesion, the devotion of a life to a system like Christianity, he manifests his maturest opinions as to its pretensions, and declares his soberest convictions as to its adaptations and merits. But when going farther, he accepts it as the one Divine provision for the wants of man, the remedy given by the Author of our being for all our woes, he binds it to his spirit and his immortality with his reason, and seals it with his faith and hope. But when going even farther yet, he is so impressed with its importance, and so persuaded of its power in all generations of men and in all climes of earth, that he feels impelled to proclaim it to the universal brotherhood as the will of God and the glad tidings of salvation, he rises into the sublimer sphere of philanthropic thought and action, and pours forth his soul under the throbbings of noblest impulse and in the currents of purest love. With such a man our author has to do, in this interesting narrative. The subject of it did not live with the expectation of having a book written to preserve his name and commemorate his deeds. He lived to serve his God, his country, the Church, the truth. He had no plan to make or spread a fame. He simply did his duty as he understood it. And from his powers of mind and his acquaintance with men and things, it was his privilege and honor to understand it well. He had carefully explored the fields of religious inquiry, and found in the Word of God the rest of his soul; and with all his heart he believed it to be the Word of Life unto all nations. Under the guidance of his Lord, it was as natural, therefore, to proclaim it unto others, as it was to embrace it for himself.

Such votes, it may be said, have always been had, and are yet given, for any and all religions in the world. The statement fails much of truth. Unquestionably there are men of good minds and sound judgment under the sway of all religions. But they could only determine according to the light given them. What is seen through a green glass *alone*, is always green. But what, viewed through various colored glasses, takes the color of the medium; and then viewed in the open light stands manifest in a hue of its own, but reveals to us that the medium is colored, and that the entire beam displays the object as it is. Men in other religions have had little opportunity of comparing one Paganism with another, and less of comparing their image-worship or hero-worship with a genuine Christianity. They have ever been dissatisfied with their systems, but have had no guide to any that are better. The moral impulse set them in motion; but flesh and sense only dragged them downwards to darkness and crime. But the case is different in Christian countries. Here intercourse is had with all nations, and all religions are open to view. When candid minds have seen the nature and the results of Christianity, they have yielded their assent; they have plighted their faith. Tribes have been educated to Christ; nations have been born in a day. Enough has been accomplished to show the superiority of the faith of the Cross. And the work is but begun.

It is not so written because we think it is a noteworthy condescension for any man, however exalted, to bow to the authority of Holy Writ; or that any man however gifted places christianity under any compliment by accepting it. The condescension, the compliment is all on the other side. The great God in condescension and love gave his Son; in condescension and love He revealed his will to man. All true. Yet on the human side there is an acceptance of the scheme, however magnificent; an admission of the provisions, however effective and glorious. And it is on this side we have the mediatorship of opinion, the high priesthood of reason. Most men do not think and determine for themselves. They accept the views the leaders of thought have elaborated, and are satisfied with the conclusions other men have reached. Personal examination of all our opinions would be a tedious matter, and would give a substitute for the basis on which the masses at present move.

Notwithstanding our boasted intelligence, prejudice and authority are yet a power among men, and ever will be. It is considerations of this kind that make it a pleasure for the christian believer to find his own faith strengthened by the faith of a good heart, a sound judgment, and a calm and robust mind. And it is also for considerations of this kind that we emphasize the hearty acceptance and faithful exemplification of christian doctrine and spirit by the veteran and the sage, the theme of our meditation.

James Richardson was a christian in the broadest sense of the term. He sought no modifications; he made no reservations. He accepted the whole scheme. And he believed it to be good for all men, and all men to be entitled to its benefits. One of the prominent characteristics of the man was the catholicity of his faith and charity of his spirit. This, no doubt, arose largely, as in all cases of genuine charity, from the directness and clearness of his views. His noble mind laid hold at once of the great essentials of the christian system, faith in Christ and obedience to the law of God. Cleaving his way with the strokes of reason and the thrusts of common sense through externals of systems and the barriers of dogma, he went at once to the heart of religion. And he took the religion of the Bible, the doctrine and the faith of the cross of Christ most earnestly to his own heart. He believed in experimental religion. He believed in no other. If there was one thing more than another that taxed his patience, it was the substitution of some device of man for the soul-converting power of God, and then calling it religion, or religious duty, or a source of religious comfort. Religion to him meant conviction of sin, a sense of guilt and helplessness, an embracing of Christ for pardon, a consequent forgiveness, peace and joy, an assurance of acceptance with God. holiness, happiness, heaven. It was a matter of the heart and life, at once the deepest and highest interest of our humanity. The idea of some millinery of the tabernacle, some ritualistic observance, some ecclesiastical imposition or form supplying the unutterable needs of the soul, cleansing and satisfying the conscience, was to him shocking and absurd. In the narration of his experience in the fellowship of the saints concerning his own conversion he often quoted the words of John Wesley : " I felt my heart strangely warmed." And upon the indwelling of the Holy Spirit, the abiding witness of the spirit, in his own oft uttered words, " the life and power of religion in the soul," he lingered with delight in his meditations, revelled in his conversation, and expatiated with triumph in his public discourse. In his quick and accurate perceptions of scripture truth, he had a perfect contempt for such notions as apostolical succession, priestly absolution, sacramental pardon or regeneration, hierarchical rule or Papal sovereignty. Through most of the many years God gave him on the earth, he stoutly resisted them, and faithfully denounced them both in public and private. Yet this was never done with the irritation or unseasonableness of the demagogue, or for the taunt and pomp of harangue, but manifestly as the result of the profoundest convictions, the solid utterances of the broadest and best intelligence. He spake so, because thus he knew and believed, and because the most precious concerns of his fellow immortals were so inextricably involved. He ever magnified the Lord Jesus Christ, His work and sacrifice. There could be no blemish in His character; no partial or total alternative for His vicarious suffering and death. No man could add aught to His atonement; none could take aught away. His was a finished work of atonement. All that accepted Him were saved. None that rejected Him could be saved. And every man might come directly to God through Him. Thus were all exalted to be kings and priests. What need then of a special line of priests? Aye, what a blasphemy, what a spoiling of Christ of His dignity and honor, that any man or any succession of men should say that to him or to them belonged the power to continue Christ's sacrifice, and perpetuate and communicate its efficacy; the power to add or diminish aught of it so as to open and shut heaven at pleasure. These and all such venerable fancies, such ecclesiastical excrescences and chronic spiritual disorders, his vigorous mind cast off with promptitude, and on the other hand asserted with boldness and clearness the vital doctrines of the Divine Word, the sovereignty of God, the priesthood of Jesus, salvation by faith alone, the immortality of the soul, and the individual accountability of man.

Furthermore, Richardson was a *Methodist*. From what has already been written it is apparent that it would be easy for him to be a Methodist, to connect himself with that great family that sprang out of the preaching and labors of John Wesley. Born and reared in the Church of England, up to manhood and till his removal from Kingston to Presque Isle, he had striven to be satisfied with the idea that a man duly baptized and receiving the sacraments is safe. Inner, heart-religion, as he himself afterward confesses, he knew not of. Resting in the outward observances, often disturbed and distressed with fears, he never knew peace, assurance, triumph, joy. Yet he was as well off as his neighbours and instructors. But there came to that early settlement on the lake, one of those restless itinerants that for over a hundred years have been pushing their way through forests, over mountains, along and across rivers, proclaiming the unsearchable riches of Christ. When James Richardson heard Wyatt Chamberlain tell what genuine religion is, he said within himself, " If this be religion I have it not." Then he sought it; he desired a heartfelt experience. His powerful and practical mind comprehended the issues of the case, and strove for the application of the remedy. He felt himself a sinner condemned under the law; then he apprehended the nature and office of Christ as he had never before done. Christ, that knew no sin, had become a sin-offering for him. Christ his substitute. He knew it, he felt it. It was then he felt his heart strangely warmed. Then he felt the principle of love and obedience take the place of pride and rebellion. He could submit to God. He did submit. He could trust the Lord and leave his ways in his Father's hand. He did trust and went forth to labor for God. Conversion, change of heart, was to him a fact, a personal experience, not dependent on a sacrament, but the resultant of confession to God and faith in Christ. Nor was it dependant on a line of priesthood, a stately ritual, or a pompous ceremonial. He was converted in a barn in a country place and among a plain people. Here he had the power of God demonstrated.

This rather upset his high church notions and well introduced him into the simplicity, majesty and efficiency of the Gospel. He was willing even to be a Methodist local preacher, in which relationship to the Church he served his Lord some five years, the time intervening from the year after his conversion, in 1818 to his entrance upon the regular itinerant work in 1824. These years of tutelage led him into a thorough acquaintance with the doctrines of grace, and prepared him in a familiarity with the economy of Methodism, with the people called Methodists, and with their religious earnestness for the important spheres of the activities of his subsequent life.

Born in 1791, the very year of the death of Wesley, thus joining in Providence his generation on Wesley's times ; early reached by the Methodist itinerants, and captivated by their spirit ; having a mind seeking out the principles of things and a nature so apt to generous influences, there is little wonder that he came to a lively appreciation of the Methodistic economy, and to a sincere love of the doctrine and discipline. Though the people called by that name were despised, he was perfectly willing to be despised with them so long as they incurred the scorn and reproach for Jesus' sake ; and the reproach was not cast upon them for irreligion or immorality ; for formalism or ritualism ; but for awakened earnestness and renewed activity, designated as these were as overwrought zeal and fanaticism. This is as though the dying flower or drooping fruit should cast reproach upon the generous life that had produced it. It were better to be alive with the lowly and the poor, than grandly coffined and magnificently sepultured with the rich and the great. The gist of the English Wesleyan movement and its extension in America was the infusion of a new spiritual power. It was not the chastening of a ritual or the expurgation of a liturgy, but the sloughing of dead integuments and the impartation of a new life. It was pre-eminently and emphatically a revival of religion. Life, life in the soul. Life in the church was its central idea. This was the excellency that arrested Richardson's attention. Again the lofty aim of the movement, to spread scriptural holiness over the land, stamped it with the patent of a heavenly nobility. "God thrust us out to raise up a holy people," said Wesley. Here was faith, courage, directness and power. Such an enterprise must have charms for a spirit given to a Christian daring and delighting in Godlike achievements. To be converted to God, to be sanctified of the Holy Ghost, and to live and labor for Jesus, this was religion to the good Bishop. Often he spake of the simple conditions of membership in Methodism as contrasted with the requirements in other churches, and of the rules of the United Societies. These more than the doctrines and methods he held to be the distinctive marks of his people. "There is only one condition previously required of those who desire admission into these societies, a desire to flee from the wrath to come and to be saved from their sins. But wherever this is really fixed in the soul it will be shown by its fruits. It is therefore expected of all who continue herein, that they should continue to evidence their desire of salvation (1) by doing no harm, by avoiding evil of every kind, (2) by doing good, (3) by attending upon the ordinances of God." Such is the catholicity of Methodism: no fettering with creeds, no persecution for opinions, no external clampings of ritual or succession. All these are adverse to its spirit. And we believe they are opposed to the spirit of the Church of Christ. We would that even all Protestant pastors apprehended these truths as clearly as James Richardson, and pronounced them as distinctly. To him the unity of the church grew up from the life within. The unity of the Church of Christ was like the unity of the vine or of the human body. It was the result of growth, compacted by that which every joint supplieth, making increase of the body unto the edifying of itself in love. How eloquently and energetically have we heard the venerable Bishop maintain these truths ! How positively would he repudiate the claims of a Hierarchy or a Papacy constructing and enforcing an external unity ! What contempt he had for all sacerdotalism and sacramentarianism attempting to weave together by human hands what God knits together with joints and bands of his own divine fabric and supply. On the other hand, what admiration he had for the spiritual and glorious unity of Christ's mystical body, the Church of God ! How diligently he labored and how constantly he pleaded for the union of all men to Christ, and in Christ. Thus he understood Christianity. Thus he understood Methodism. Wherefore it was the one employment of his best abilities, the one aim of his best efforts to make Methodism a power in the land.

Furthermore, he was an Episcopal Methodist. And this he was right heartily and loyally, and of an immovable conviction. He never was a sectary or bigot, of such a character in his noble charity he was utterly incapable. But among all christian denominations he preferred Episcopal Methodism. And to it was he affectionately devoted from the day of his conversion to God till the day of his death. His attachments grew with his years, and strengthened with his enlarging experience. When he was converted the Methodists of the country were, with scarcely an exception, all episcopal. In 1790, the year before his birth, Wm. Losee, of the New York Conference of the Methodist Episcopal Church, under the direction of Asbury, introduced Methodism into Canada. On the appointment of the same apostolic bishop and his coadjutor, itinerant followed itinerant into those northern wilds, looking up the settler as he penetrated the forests and planted his home along our lakes and bays. Bangs, Jewell, Dunham, Pickett, Sawyer, Ryan, Case, and many contemporaries and successors were sent in from the New York Conferences, the Bay Quinte district and Niagara district, being considered as regularly part of their work as the districts about Albany and New York. And why should it not be so? Why should the catholic kingdom of Jesus Christ be hemmed in or divided by political boundaries? Why should the petty strifes of men mark out the limits of the Church of God? In 1811 Asbury himself made an episcopal tour of Canada. At this time there were two districts, eleven circuits, and nearly three thousand members. In 1817, about the time of Richardson's removal from Kingston to Presque Isle, the Genesee annual conference of the Methodist Episcopal Church was held at Elizabethtown, near Brockville, under presidency of Bishop George, and in 1820 the same conference under the same presidency was held in the chapel at the west end of Lundy's Lane. By this time the circuits had grown to seventeen in number and the membership to nearly 6,000. In August 1824, Bishops George and Hedding were both present at the organization of the Canada Conference, as an annual Conference of the M. E. Church; and the latter presided in October 1828, in the Ernestown conference when the Canada conference organized itself into an independent "Methodist Episcopal Church in Canada." At the request of the conference he also presided at Kingston in 1830, and ordained, as presented to him, six elders and twenty-one deacons. The American Bishops of course presided over the conferences intervening between 1824 and 1828.

Richardson passed through all these scenes; with many of them he was closely connected, and in them a chief actor. He had, therefore, every opportunity of observing the operations of this polity. Likewise he was early predisposed in its favor from his nurture in the Church of England. At the Saltfleet Conference in 1825, Bishop Hedding in the chair, Jas. Richardson and Egerton Ryerson were admitted on trial. Under this economy he travelled with William Case, William, John and Egerton Ryerson, Thos. Madden, Anson Green, Philander Smith, and others whose names are familiar in the early Methodism of the country. In 1827 Ryerson and Richardson were ordained deacons by bishop Hedding in the old church yet standing on King street, Hamilton; and in 1830, they and others made up the list of six elders. Several times secretary of the conference up to 1832, he had cherished this economy, and as editor of the *Christian Guardian*, established in the interests of the M. E. Church in Canada, he had defended it. No wonder then that his mind recoiled from the measures of the conference in 1833, that swept away at one stroke, bishops, elders, and deacons, annual and general conferences, and adopted an annual conference of ministers in lieu thereof. No wonder that he and others resisted to the last the casting away of the organization and polity deliberately recommended by John Wesley to the churches in America and the taking instead thereof, the distorted institutions and undesirable expediencies into which that good man had been forced in Britain, cramped and crowded as was the growth of his societies by state requirements and the oppressive domination of the Established Church. No wonder good men saddened, and doubted, and waited and wavered and wept and prayed. If there is anything that intelligent and true men come to love, it is not first, hill, or river, or mountain, but it is first, and deepest, and longest, and strongest, the precious ordinances, appointments, and agencies of the Church, and the cherished institutions of the State, these institutions that save our life, guard our liberties, instruct our minds, and purify our hearts, increase our comforts, bless our kindred, and exalt our race ; these are our dearest inheritance and our best legacy to our children. In such an honored rank was the Canadian Methodist Episcopacy previous to 1833. So did many of the fathers cherish it, and so do many of their children love it to-day. So is it venerated and held by millions of the Methodists of the United States of America this hour. They would rather you would take their homes than the ecclesiastical economy recommended to them under the sanctions of history by the wise and venerable Wesley, and adopted with Coke's and Asbury's ordinations by the general conference of 1784. It is to them a bond of union and a fortress of power. It is a pledge of security, of progress and of peace. Such an estimate did Richardson and several of his contemporaries place upon it. Who shall wonder that he was in consternation, in difficulty and doubt, when it was swept away? The wonder is that he did not promptly, openly, boldly and continually resist the destruction of such a polity. This is the one mistake of his life. He and others of the time that loved these institutions ought to have rallied to their defence. The face of affairs would have been different to-day. But as the noble bishop often said: "They acted in the interests of harmony and peace; and they thought they did for the best." And so may it be in the Providence of God. Who can tell? For peace' sake he went for a little with the tide, and then for his own peace and conscience' sake he sought another course and turned the shattered keel into the old channels and the well-known waters. Sweeping over the well charted track his vessel at length made happy port in full sail. There was administered unto him an abundant entrance.

He and those with him found Canada to be peculiarly the suffering ground of Episcopal Methodism. Inasmuch as at civil suggestion and outside ecclesiastical interference, the many would abdicate and even abrogate the polity the few desired, its maintenance became a matter of vital importance. Episcopacy became a centre of contention; its defence and promotion a principal of action. It would not therefore be a matter of surprise if some of its aspects had been unduly magnified, if there had been over-estimates and exaggerations touching it. Too much may have been said about the orders and too little store set by the proclamation of God's Word by men not very regular or defensible in their orders. Yet a solid mind like Richardson's having had the advantage of all the experience and history of the contest must take in all the issues of the case and must pronounce a verdict worthy of respect. And when that verdict has the sanction of a life of privation and suffering, like the testimony of the Apostles, it is the more to be regarded. Just as the acceptance of the Gospel by intellects of a certain grade and habit is an argument for the Gospel, so the adoption and retention of a polity by minds of power and of opportunities for experience is an argument in favor of the polity. And Richardson did, unreservedly and unqualifiedly, accept the Methodist Episcopacy. While on the one hand he rejected, as an invention of man, the divine right of the Episcopacy, and the conveyance of authority or sacramental force and virtue in a line of succession from the Apostles, on the other he held fast and firm the doctrine of a divine call to the Ministry, and the necessity of a proper recognition of the call by the Church of God, in formal and public acceptance of the candidate and in his solemn designation to his office. And inasmuch as the Apostles had instituted their Churches with the grades or orders of Bishop or Elder, and Deacon, and these arrangements of men had been sanctioned in New Testament times by the Spirit of God, and inasmuch as high evangelical authorities through successive ages, had called back the Church from arrogant assumptions to Apostolical simplicity; and especially as John Wesley, convinced of the validity of Episcopal ordinances, as opposed to Papal or Hierarchical, had so organized the Church in America, it did seem important to Richardson and many of his associates in the Conference, that the Episcopacy, as given them by Mr. Wesley, should be retained. They therefore resisted to the last in the Conference the proposed changes, and when these had been consummated, they acquiesced for a little to avoid rending the Church. In this spirit and yet ill at ease, Richardson acted with the Conference for a time, and at length withdrew, and even took work in the United States, thinking that in the Christian Ministry under the cherished Episcopacy, he would find some compensation for a temporary absence from his native land. But here operated another strong principle of his nature. His love of country and devotion to the Crown made him restless in his associations with a people, however intelligent, pious and worthy, that did not sympathize with the strong emotions of his soul, or hold their ordinary conversation in harmony with his views on governmental order and public policy. Seeking again the rest he had crossed the national lines to obtain, he speedily returned to Canada. Here he found a band of Episcopal Methodists that had never left their Church or submitted to an unconstitutional abandonment of the Episcopacy, doing what had been better done by himself and those that hesitated with him in the day of crisis and calamity. They were rallying about the old standard and had determined to maintain Episcopal Methodism in the country, though fiercely assailed from both political and ecclesiastical quarters. With them, though the prospect was in all conscience forbidding enough, Richardson decided to cast in his lot, and take what might come, trusting in the Lord. Obloquy did come, and much gainsaying and persecution, but his convictions were deep and firm, and here his settled mind had rest. He had associated himself with a church, comparatively weak it is true; but then he had a people ready to suffer in the interests of their country, to deny themselves of Government patronage in vindication of the voluntary principle of Church support; a people to whom the simple Word of God was a delight, and the Episcopal polity given of Wesley and sanctioned of the fathers was a rallying point and a fortress. And with this people he laboured and suffered till death brought him to his reward.

For some years, with the consent of his Conference, he served the Upper Canada Bible Society. His efficiency in that sphere is well attested by the eulogies and records on the occasion of his death. In 1858 at St. Davids he was elected and consecrated Bishop of the Methodist Episcopal Church in Canada. This office gave fitting scope to his magnificent powers of administration. His were endowments that would have shone in a councillor of state or a judge upon the bench. Yet they were ever employed in all meekness and gentleness with the evident desire to promote the interests of his church and bring glory to God. In knowledge of ecclesiastical law and usage he had no superior in the land. In Methodist polity and discipline he was as thoroughly versed as any man of his times. Having acted as exhorter, local preacher, assistant, preacher in charge, and presiding elder he had regularly graduated in this great university of evangelism and grace. To regulate the affairs of circuits and districts, to direct the movements of the itinerancy, to guide and control the deliberations and enterprises of conferences, and with dignity and effect to preside in boards and senates seemed to him like a second nature, and never apparently either burdened or perplexed him. Under a weight of responsibility he was steady; amid conflicting opinions he was calm, and in the agitations of assemblies he was easy and firm. He brought the coolness and promptness of the naval chieftan, qualities he had disciplined in actual service, into the storms of councils and the commotions of conferences. His advanced years even at the time he entered upon the duties of the episcopate, left not much to be expected at his hands in the line of personal supervision of the vast field by actual visitation of the charges: Nevertheless he was much abroad in the work, and wherever he moved, his sincere piety, his weight of character, the breadth of his experience, the extent of his wisdom, the gentility of his bearing and the unaffected simplicity of his manner rendered him powerful for good in any circle he touched, and gave him the high honor of being at once a godly man and a universal favourite among the people.

Among all his countrymen of all religious denominations he was held in veneration, and they vied one with the other in proffering the kindliest of offices and paying the profoundest respect. He was entertained at many homes of those not of his own people, and had among his sincerest friends and admirers those that belonged to other ecclesiastical communions. Even the rulers of the land waited upon his conversation with profit, for, for him to tell his experience was to recite the history and unfold the policy of former times. He knew by sight and feeling and personal intercourse what they were learning from books. In the families of his charge all were impressed that the venerable bishop had a solemn mission, and saw that he was about the Master's business. Yet all felt they had free access to him, and were lifted by his example and conversation to the purer intercourse of heaven. To the children of the households he visited he was always joyously welcome; to the youth it was a delight to serve him, and to the mature and aged his recitals of incident and interchanges of opinion were always an opportunity and an honor. He was thought in all respects a model Bishop, and any one going by the name must be like him in person and act. His successor was at a certain place voted out of the office by the juveniles because he had two arms. "He could not be a Bishop for Bishop Richardson had only one arm." And he was indeed a model Bishop. They are rare that have as well filled up the outlines of the Apostolical pattern: "A Bishop must be blameless, the husband of one wife, vigilant, sober, of good behaviour, given to hospitality, apt to teach, not given to wine, no striker, not greedy of filthy lucre, but patient, not a brawler, not covetous; not a novice, lest being lifted up with pride, he fall into condemnation of the devil. Moreover he must have a good report from them that are without, lest he fall into reproach and the snares of the devil."

Viewed simply as a preacher of the gospel the subject of our narrative presented points of interest. His forte was argument; calm, consecutive reasoning. His propositions were definite and their logical connection clear. His exposition of Scripture at once edified and satisfied the mind. There was no effort at ornamentation of style, and yet his discourse was far from being without ornament. There was never an attempt at moving the feelings without first convincing the judgment, and yet often his auditors, in sympathy with himself, were melted to tears. In preaching he ordinarily opened with a lucid statement of the Scriptural connections of his theme. His divisions were distinct and his proofs of what he attempted decisive, and when argument had culminated into persuasion, and persuasion into entreaty, he bore along with him the convictions and emotions of the hearers. The love of God to man, as manifested in Christ's humiliation, passion and crucifixion was to him the melting theme, and when his heart glowed under the beams of this love, the train of argument had been so well laid that the flame ran swiftly to all hearts and melted all into contrition and sacred joy. What shouts have leaped from other lips while his have quivered with trembling and overflowing utterance! It is not enough to affirm, "God so loved the world that he gave his only begotten Son," majestic as is the enunciation. It is not enough to sweep into rhapsody or swell into declamation on the infinite benevolence of Jehovah, or His eternal purposes of goodness. The attention must be detained at length on the magnificent theme. The hearer must behold the wonders of His law, the glories of His government and the riches of His grace. He must contemplate the mysteries of redemption, the worth of the soul, and the inestimable price paid for it in blood. Thus to detain the mind and unfold the marvels of grace was our preacher's delight and strength. It was by these presentations in plain yet forcible and majestic speech, that he kindled the emotions and bare upward the flame till his audience was swept in thought and feeling to the light-crowned eminences of truth and duty.

Again, it was a matter of emphasis with him, likely more than with any of his brethren, to denounce in fearless tone, yet in dispassionate and effective terms, all formalism, and ritualism and sacerdotalism in the Church of the Living God. Detesting sham everywhere, he could not for a moment bear it in religion. In his view, man was born with a corrupt nature; had incurred the guilt of actual sin; if in sin, was lying every hour under the flashing condemnation of God's law; could not deliver himself; was weak, helpless, utterly unworthy; must have an atonement, a Saviour, or forever perish; could not redeem his brother; could find no help in man or angel. God, God alone could bring salvation; God's Son, very God, our Lord Jesus Christ, alone could effect atonement. He is our High Priest, and He alone. There is no pardon but through his blood. There is no cleansing but His blood applied by the Eternal Spirit. There is no mediator, no altar, no sacrifice, no priest, but the lowly Nazarene on the Cross of Calvary, the exalted Redeemer at the right hand of God. Through Him and Him alone men have access to God. By him alone they have pardon, life, and power to keep the divine commands. The era of typical priest, and altar and ceremony is gone and the true light now shineth. We must be born again, born of the Spirit, and live in the obedience of love through faith. The sacrament has no saving, converting, cleansing power in itself; and is but the sign of reconciliation already effected, and allegiance already sworn. A new heart given of God on repentance and faith, must be the spring of a new life wrought out in the man by the Holy Ghost, and by the man in his bringing forth the fruits of the Spirit. To a mind imbued with such views of the essence and character of the Christian religion as a transaction betwixt God and the soul through Jesus Christ alone, how must the claims of the Papacy appear; the arrogance of the so-called priesthood, the imputed efficacy of the sacraments, or the asserted spiritual energy of certain forms. Contemptible! all contemptible, and always contemptible! Aye, more and worse than that! A monstrosity of crime and wickedness, since they are employed by the proud, the corrupt, the selfish and the sinful to delude the masses of men, and keep them in blindness and ignorance that they and their substance may be used for the gratification of lust, and at the behest of hierarchical avarice and ambition. In view of these misled and perishing multitudes, our preacher's generous soul was filled with indignation and sadness. He could not but be indignant that these assumptions that had wrought such ruin in the past, were still flaring and exulting in the ranks of the wordly and the haughty that are readiest to call themselves the Church of God. He could not but be sad that under the guise and name of religion, so many were benighted and led on through sin to death. Indignant and sad, it was the burden of his ministry eloquently to proclaim against such a priesthood, the fallacy and wickedness of such assumptions, and eloquently to advocate in the face of the people, the perfection of Christ's atonement and the sufficiency and infallibility of the Word of God.

It may be fitting to conclude this paper, by a glance at the world-ward side of the subject of our sketch. If James Richardson was a man of God, he was also a man for the world. If he was a preacher of divine truth he was also an advocate and defender of the rights of man. If he was a Bishop in the church of Christ, he was also a prince in the Commonwealth of freemen; one of the kingliest in a nation of kings. He was a living illustration that religion is not one thing, and the social bond, or civil obligation, or political duty quite another. Man is held to man by various ties; but the divine bond, religion, that holds all men one to the other, and all men to the great God, runs a silken cord throughout the whole warp and woof and is that alone that gives integrity and endurance to the entire fabric. The separation of religion from domestic or civil or social duties is a perfect absurdity. It is that divorcement of what God has joined together that curses the human race. There is no such thing as duty at all, unless there is the eternal throne and the Almighty God enthroned thereon. It is because God made us, and made us free and morally intelligent that we are accountable. This is the source of law and sanction of government and judgment and penalty: and this for all life's relations is religion, the bond and the obligation of all intelligent and free creatures to the eternal throne. The true citizen then is loyal at once to his God and his King. There is no sounder philosophy, no purer religion than this: " Honor all men, love the brotherhood, fear God, honor the

King." Of this philosophy and this religion the venerable Bishop through all his days was a noble exemplification. He learned loyalty of his father, a veteran mariner in the British service. Himself a sailor in very childhood, at the early age of 18 he entered the royal marines on the lakes. A lieutenant in the navy he served his king and country in the war of 1812, and distinguished himself by his valor and discretion on several occasions of importance. He bore to his death an evidence of the determination and courage with which he prosecuted the attack upon Oswego, in that with one hand alone he was compelled to indicate the way of duty to men, and with one arm alone to fight the remainder of life's battles. He was ever devoutly attached to the British throne, and cherished the profoundest reverence for the British constitution, usages and laws. He intelligently and conscientiously preferred them above all the polities of other nations, and all the institutes and orders of other governments of the earth. He held to the crown and the throne firmly enough for the staunchest Tory: he contended for the rights of the people strenuously enough, and swept away the tyrannies of orders and aristocracies ruthlessly enough for the most radical Reformer. Born in 1791, the very year that Upper Canada was made a chartered colony and given an organization in government by George III., he grew up through our history and participated in the political movements of his times. Drawn by some of his kinsmen into politics before he entered the gospel ministry, he never ceased to take a lively interest in the public affairs of the country. With all the early Methodists he was fervently opposed to every form and degree of Church and State connection that in any way hampered the Church with the bonds of the State ; and it was this settled conviction of his mind, and this unalterable determination of his public policy, that decided his course in the years and events of the disruption of Canadian Methodism. He could give no countenance to a movement that was to divert his people from their long settled principles and betray their political influence into the hands of a party striving to the very death to make the Church of England the established Church of Canada, and renew in the Province the oppression and wrongs, the spiritual inactivity and unfruitfulness of the establishment in the mother land. These statements will also readily indicate what course he would pursue in the settlement of those angry questions that pivoted on the rectories, the clergy reserves, King's College and Toronto University, and all kindred issues before the country. In every conflict he was with the people and opposed to any and every ecclesiastical or political aristocracy and monopoly. He firmly and fully believed that every man should be free to worship God according to the dictates of his conscience, should be protected by the laws of the land therein, and should not be compelled directly or indirectly by taxation to support another's peculiar dogma or creed. Liberty of conscience and liberty of worship were cardinal doctrines of his religious and political faith. The voluntary principle, the support of every Church's institutions by the contributions of its members and adherents or friends in harmony with its spirit was a favorite rallying cry of his co-religionists and a cherished aim of his heart and life for his beloved native land. Though never meddling in party strifes, or interfering in sectional or partisan conflicts, he was always well informed on the great issues before the people and prepared with hand and voice to act his part. At home in the political movements of all countries, he was profoundly interested in everything that pertained to his own land and people. He loved his country ardently and served it honorably and faithfully, and for that love and service he was dearly beloved by his countrymen. Few men have filled out so well the orb of a perfect character; and few have been permitted of God to shine out so long and so bright amid the constellations of this lower firmament. Lifted high in the empyrean he still sheds through the spheres a mild radiance on the world. In the mystic photography of the soul, the gentle ray in silent energy is tracing out the lineaments of his character and the record of his life on the walls and pillars of the living temple, reared of living stones; and as they come forth to our view and shine out among men, we read that he that hath gone up from the earth was one of nature's noblemen, a true man, a brother indeed, a christian, patriot, sage.

CHAPTER I.

Birth—Parentage—Father's services under Lord Rodney in Royal Navy—Imminent danger—Loss of the Ramillies in a storm—Taken prisoner and carried to France—After the close of the war, sent to Canada—Connection with the Canadian Marine—Shipwreck on Lake Ontario—Chased by American vessels during the war of 1812—Mother's early Life in America—Incidents.

Rev. James Richardson, D.D., late Bishop of the Methodist Episcopal Church in Canada, was born in Kingston, Upper Canada, January 29th, 1791, and died at his residence, Clover Hill, Toronto, March 9th, 1875, being in the 85th year of his age, and 51st of his ministry. Bishop Richardson was of English parentage. His father was one of those "who went down to the sea in ships, to do business in great waters." Respecting him the late Bishop remarks:

"My father was a native of Lincolnshire, England, and followed the sea. He was in the Royal Navy attached to the Ramillies, 74, one of the fleet under Lord Rodney, in the

West Indies in 1782, and which after the defeat of the French fleet under De Grasse, formed part of the convoy to a large fleet of merchantmen with the prizes taken in the action."

Bishop Carman in the funeral discourse delivered in the Metropolitan Church, Toronto, on the occasion of the late Bishop's death, remarked on the same subject:

" His father served under Admiral Rodney in his splendid victories over the French and Spanish fleets, during the continuance of the Revolutionary war, and shared in that great conflict in the West Indies, on the 12th of April, 1782, in which the French naval armament under Count De Grasse, was well nigh annihilated."

As we have already seen, after Lord Rodney's victory over De Grasse, the Ramillies, with several other men of war, set sail for England as a convoy to the prizes which had been taken. The royal fleet had successfully bid defiance to the shot and shell of the French and Spanish armies, and had obtained a decisive victory. They were now destined to encounter a more terrible enemy, in opposition to whom courage and military skill were unavailing. In relation to this Bishop Richardson says:

"Homeward bound, the British fleet encountered the celebrated hurricane which sent to the bottom of the Atlantic most of the men of war. The Ramillies after losing her masts, and throwing her guns overboard, then in a sinking condition, buffeted by the storm for five days, went down, her officers and crew happily escaping in some of the merchant vessels. So violent was this storm that the fleet was separated, while the crews of many of the vessels, less fortunate than those of the Ramillies, went down with their ships."

"I have frequently heard my father relate the particulars of the awfully perilous situation of the men on the Ramillies, during the five days of their fearful suspense. Many were the expedients resorted to in order to keep the ship afloat till the gale should subside. Incessant pumping and other labours were continued, at which old Admiral Greaves himself worked, to encourage others to take their turn."

The crew of the Ramillies had however but escaped one calamity to be overtaken by another, the merchantman and crew being immediately afterwards captured by an American frigate. Mr. Richardson, the father of the late Bishop, was with his companions in arms, taken to France, and kept there till the return of peace.

After his release in 1785, he came to Quebec in the service of King George the Third. Subsequently he was appointed to office in the Canadian Marine on the lakes and rivers in these provinces. His official position in this service brought him to Kingston, where he afterwards located his family. In company with other noble pioneer settlers in Upper Canada, the Richardson family experienced numerous hardships, incident to a life in the wilderness. They were however comparatively free from the bitter privations which some of the earlier and less fortunate settlers had to endure. Mrs. Richardson especially had to suffer many discomforts, besides being subject to much anxiety of mind, during the lengthened absence of her husband on the lakes. For several weeks at a time it would be impossible for her to gain reliable information concerning him, sometimes months would intervene before he would be heard from. Those were the days when men sought wild adventure for their country's good, and women suffered in silence and were strong.

Captain Richardson was fond of the water and preferred to plow the boisterous billows with the keel of his ship, rather than encounter the primeval forests, and use the "shovel plow" among the stumps and roots of the newly cleared lands.

A few years after the termination of the American Revolution, the people in the vicinity of Kingston, and along the shores of the Bay of Quinte, opened up a trade in grain with the American soldiers at Fort Oswego, and the people of that part of the state of New York. Captain Richardson became engaged in this trade as well as in other branches of business which could be carried on upon the lakes.

The following brief allusion to one of Captain Richardson's trips to Oswego, is from the pen of the late Bishop, as sent to the writer some years since.

"The following incident in the life of my father serves to show the dangers and difficulties attendant on the communication by water between places near each other, though upon opposite sides of the lake. As late as 1795 or 1796 the American troops at Fort Oswego had to look to Canada for flour, and my father contracted to furnish a supply in the fall of the year, just previous to the setting in of winter. He took in his cargo, purchased of the families along the Bay of Quinte, and sailed for Oswego; but just at the mouth of the river encountered a severe wind which baffled all attempt at making harbour. (No steam power for navigation purposes in those days.) Being driven into the lake, and a furious snow-storm ensuing, he was driven, after combating all night with the wind, waves, and snow, into the mouth of Sandy Creek and wrecked, being now between twenty and thirty miles east of Oswego.

My father, and a seaman who was with him, swam to shore, but here was only snow and woods. No friendly roof to shelter them, no food to satisfy the cravings of hunger, nor fire to warm the poor benumbed limbs, and no settlement short of Oswego to the north, and a reported commencement of one called Rotterdam, about fifteen miles through dense woods and swamps, to the southward. They first tried the woods, but sinking above the knees in snow and slush they had to abandon that route, and take the course of the lake shore to Oswego, intersected as it was by several streams. They commenced their journey, as already intimated, without food or fire.

Providence however was kind to them in the time of their greatest necessity, for on arriving at the mouth of the Salmon River, twelve or fifteen miles east of Oswego, they discovered a boat with her crew on the opposite side, storm bound in the creek. They called and were immediately brought over and relieved. My father proceeded with the boat to Oswego, as soon as possible, and reported the total loss of his vessel and cargo. Winter having now set in, and navigation closed for the season, he had no way left of returning home but by Schenectady, or Albany, and thence by lake Champlain and Lower Canada to Kingston. His home was not reached before the month of February. My mother in the mean time at Kingston, had heard nothing of him further than that his vessel was wrecked, the cargo lost, and that he had reached Salmon River, and had gone from thence to Oswego. Judge of her anxiety, alone with her little family during those dreary months, till my father's return."

This incident may be taken as a sample of the disasters and dangers incident upon travelling in those days. However, Captain Richardson was not the man to be disheartened. Having decided to push his business as vigorously as ever, before the lake was free from ice in the spring he was again making ready for the lake trade.

Another incident which will illustrate the character of the man for courage and perseverance, was related to the writer, by the late

Bishop, while sailing amid the scenes of the adventure.

During the war of 1812, Captain Richardson having been up Lake Ontario with his schooner, the "Simcoe," on some transport service, was passing down, and when nearing Kingston, was intercepted by American war vessels and signalled to "lie to," an order which was disregarded by the intrepid old man. Being determined that his vessel should not fall into the hands of the enemy, his first thought was to run her ashore and burn her, but while preparing to carry out his intention a breeze sprang up, and it being favorable for a run into port, he proposed to his men that they should attempt it. The men readily acquiesced, the canvas was crowded on, and everything arranged with alacrity, the men being as prompt to obey as the captain was to give the order.

The Americans were quick to discover Richardson's intention of running past them and immediately fired a shot at the vessel, which fortunately did no harm. The captain had given his men orders in case they should be struck in the hull, to be ready to take prompt measures to prevent the water, as far as possible, from flowing into the schooner. The vessel was kept to her course in the most gallant style, hugging the shore as closely as possible, her lighter draught enabling her to run much nearer the shore than the pursuing Americans dared to come. The chase was a hot one; the enemy with all his canvas spread bearing down upon the schooner and pouring shot after shot into her with fearful effect. The water was now rushing in through the battered sides of the vessel, but the men at the pumps were vigorous and worked with a will. The chase was viewed from the shore, the most intense excitement prevailing on every side, not only on account of the "Simcoe," but as to what might be the subsequent course of the Americans. Soon, to the great joy of the spectators it was perceived that Richardson had run his vessel past his assailants, and had gained a point which rendered further pursuit impracticable, the enemy not daring to venture within range of the guns of the fort. And now amidst the most enthusiastic cheers of his anxious friends on the shore, the gallant officer ran his shattered vessel into port; and as he did so he gave the discomfited enemy a parting salute by firing off an old musket.

Captain Richardson had, however, just reached the port in time. The vessel was in a sinking condition, and the men had scarcely left her ere she went down.* We now turn our attention for a time from the adventurous father to the not less heroic mother of the subject of this memoir.

Mrs. Richardson, whose maiden name was Sarah Asmore, was born in Kingsnorton, a small but ancient town not far from Birmingham, England. Prior to the American Revolution, while yet a young woman, she came to America with the family of Mr. John Stedman, who settled in the province of New York, on the banks of the Niagara River, at or near Fort Schlosser.

---

* Wishing to have his memory refreshed, the author wrote to Dr. Richardson for information concerning this adventure of Captain Richardson, but his reply did not arrive till after the above was written. Dr. Richardson's account is however substantially the same.

We have not been able to ascertain the precise time when Mr. Stedman settled above the Falls, but he resided at Fort Schlosser when Sir William Johnson took Fort Niagara from the French on the 24th of July, 1759, as will be seen hereafter.

The fragments of Miss Asmore's history with which we have become acquainted, indicate that she possessed a vigorous intellect, with great energy of character and courage, and she appears also to have largely imbibed the spirit of adventure so rife in those days of frontier life. It is now considerably more than a hundred years since this English maiden first heard the roaring cataract, and saw its mighty masses of waters tumbling and plunging into the deep abyss beneath, with all the grandeur and sublimity of its pristine surroundings. We can imagine the fair stranger, fresh from her quiet transatlantic home, standing beside the rapids, as the immense sheet of water, reflecting the sun's rays like a mirror, swept with inconceivable rapidity before her vision, without a ripple on its smooth surface until the mighty flowing flood dashed suddenly over the Horseshoe falls down the deep gorge into the boiling, yawning gulf below, and went thundering among those awe-inspiring, everlasting rocks, sending back to the clouds in its fearful leap a volume of spray, which, in its turn was to be transformed by the rays of the sun into the glorious bow that set its signet of beauty to the whole scene. The voice of many waters thus sounding in her ears may have reminded her of the Great Creator of the universe who so impressively manifested Himself in His works. Did she behold with rapturous delight the majestic forests that fringed the beautiful Niagara, from Lake Erie to where the pure waters of the river are lost in Lake Ontario? Or did the solemn depths of the wilderness impress her with a sense of mysterious awe?

The scenery about Niagara Falls one hundred and twenty-five years ago was more stupendously magnificent than it is now—grand as it is even yet—for nature was then in her primeval glory; and yet the banks of that river with all their awe-inspiring native grandeur witnessed scenes of carnage and bloody strife, soul sickening in their details. Here the pale face and the red man met in deadly conflict, the French and English leading on the European and Provincial battalions, each aided by their savage allies.

The members of Mr. Stedman's household were often the unwilling spectators of these encounters, Mr. Stedman himself sometimes taking an active part in them. In consequence of Mrs. Richardson's residence in the contested border-land during the French war, her mind was stored with legends of the many appalling deeds of horror perpetrated in those times along the New York frontier.

Immediately after Sir William Johnson defeated the French and had obtained possession of Fort Niagara, the British above the Falls, on the New York side of the river, were anxious to communicate with him, but the woods about the "Old Landing," now called Lewiston, were infested with the French soldiers and their Indian allies, who having escaped from Johnson were thirsting for revenge.

The following item extracted from the manuscript of the late Bishop may not be uninteresting to the reader : " Some of these parental traditions may not be out of place as they evince some of the features of those early days, and the life and death struggles of those who lived on the then western frontier of the New York colony. After the capture of Fort Niagara by Sir William Johnson, the east bank of the river was beset with hordes of hostile Indians and French, who infested the woods between Forts Niagara and Schlosser, so that all communication was intercepted for a time. The authorities offered a grant of the carrying place or portage, consisting of the monopoly of the transport service and trade, between the head of navigation on the Niagara at the " Old Landing,"—Lewiston and Schlosser—to any man who would carry a despatch from Schlosser to Niagara. Mr. Stedman undertook the task accompanied by an officer of the army. Both being mounted on fleet horses, they rode the fierce gauntlet, the Indians and French firing on them from the woods on either side. The officer was shot dead, but Stedman escaped and carried the despatch safely through." The Indians after this adventure gave to Mr. Stedman the name of the "Alligator," holding him in "superstitious reverence," believing him to be invulnerable to a bullet.

The Bishop continues: "Another incident of that war, received by tradition from my mother, was the entire massacre and destruction of a detachment of the British by the French and Indians at a certain spot on the old river road, between the "Old Landing" and the Falls, known to this day as the Devil's Hole, which is a deep gorge in the bank of the river over the head of which a log bridge extended. Here the enemy lay in ambush, and suddenly springing on their prey consisting of men, women, and children, with teams and wagons, either killed or precipitated them off the bridge, and left them to perish in the gorge. The bridge from this disaster got the name of the "Bloody Bridge."

In process of time Miss Asmore was married to Lieutenant Bryant of the "King's Navy on the lakes and rivers, designated the Provincial Marine." He was appointed to the command of a vessel named the Charity. On one occasion the vessel ran upon a shoal of rocks off the entrance to Carleton Island channel, at the foot of Lake Ontario, and it was with much difficulty that it was saved from becoming a total wreck. The rocks have ever since been known among lake navigators as the "Charity Shoal." "This shoal is surrounded by very deep water, distant several miles from any land, and is nearly mid channel as vessels pass from the lake to the river St. Lawrence. Consequently in former years when the level of the water in the lakes and rivers was six or seven feet lower than it has been at any time since 1818, it was considered a dangerous spot and an object of much anxiety to sailors passing that way in a dark night or in foggy weather, there being no beacon or light by which to make the passage."

"While my mother was Mrs. Bryant," the bishop proceeds, "she resided at Navy Hall, a marine barrack on the margin of the Niagara, on the Canadian side, near the old Fort

George. Here she was for a long time the only white woman on that side of the river, and while her husband was away on duty, she would be at times surrounded by thousands of savages, often revelling in drunkenness and war dances, it being the period of the American Revolutionary war. Yet they seldom troubled her, and only in one instance was she threatened with personal violence. She was, on this occasion, preparing some food for her dinner. Two Indians entered the house, and one of them being in a drunken state, demanded the food Mrs. Byrant was cooking. She refused to give it up, whereupon the fellow drew his knife, but his arm was arrested by his more sober companion, who dragged the offender from the house and led him away. My mother following them to the door, and observing a captain of one of the king's vessels coming along, informed against the Indian; upon which the Captain, using his sword-belt gave the fellow a sound beating on his bare back, his companion the meantime pleading for mercy on his behalf."

At the termination of the revolutionary war and upon the return of peace, the forces were reduced. Mr. Bryant and Mr. Lyons who had served in the 8th regiment located on adjacent lands situated on a small stream which empties its waters into the Chippawa, a few miles from the place where the latter river empties into the Niagara. This creek is called Lyons' creek to this day.

Prior to the location of their lands in the same vicinity, the families of Mr. Bryant and Mr. Lyons had formed an intimate acquaintance, and a friendship sprang up between them which continued without abatement through life. Mrs. Bryant and Mrs. Lyons during the military career of their husbands, had been for a length of time the only white women in that vicinity, so that they very naturally became much attached to each other.

The attempt to make homes for themselves at Lyons' creek was not successful, for neither the gallant soldier nor the fearless sailor knew much about clearing land, or farming it after it had been cleared, and therefore, the respective families, during the time that they resided there, endured all the hardships incident to early pioneer life, without reaping any corresponding benefit.

Mr. Bryant died soon after settling on his land, and thus his wife was left to struggle alone as best she could with the difficulties of the situation, her children—two sons—being too young at the time of their father's death, to be anything more than an additional charge to her.

Subsequently, (we are not furnished with the date) Lieutenant Richardson was married to Mrs. Bryant, and removed to Kingston, where Mr. Richardson took up his residence.

From the families of the Lyons', Bryants', and Richardsons', have sprung numerous and respectable descendants, many of whom have continued to make their homes in the highly favored land of their birth; while others of them having removed to the United States, have been equally esteemed as worthy and honored citizens of that republic.

But, in a brief memoir like this, we have not space to enter into further details concerning the courage, heroism, and persistent endurance of the elder Mr. Richardson and his wife, and their more intimate connections. Interesting as further particulars might be, we are compelled to turn from the exploits of the parent to those of the son.

CHAPTER II.

Promising Childhood—Moral and Religious Training—Fondness for the water—Attention to navigation and topography of our lake and river shores and channels—Enters the service—His character—Receives a commission in 1812—Changes in 1813—Continues in the service—Unsuccessful attempt on Sackett's Harbour—An expedition—Treachery—Burning of "Big Sodus"—Battle of Oswego—Loss of his arm—Subsequent disaster—Commendatory notice—Sir James L. Yeo's certificate.

The young James Richardson from his childhood gave pleasing promise of both a comely and a brave manhood. He possessed an erect frame, and an open, handsome countenance. And it was early evident that he was also endowed with a clear and strong intellect, which his parents were desirous he should cultivate and store with useful knowledge; therefore they gave him the benefit of such opportunities for acquiring an education as the country then afforded.

His father and mother were members of the Church of England, and his early religious impressions were received from that body, strengthened by home training and instruction; love of truth and honesty, and a sense of honor and of duty were engraved upon his heart long before he made a public profession of experimental religion. His reverence for the Bible, and for the gospel truths contained therein never wavered, even when exposed to the temptations incident to a military life. Moral integrity and manly dignity were marked features in his long and eventful career.

His regular school-life, which he used to advantage, making creditable progress, for his age, closed when he was about thirteen years old; but having a fixed purpose to increase his stock of knowledge, he devoted himself as circumstances permitted to useful study, and thus became familiar with the best works on theology and general literature to be found in the language.

Inheriting his father's fondness for the water, and perhaps also his love of adventure, he commenced his career as a sailor in 1804, going out in his father's vessel. Captain Richardson being an experienced seaman, and the youthful

James being anxious to excel in the art of navigation, made such good use of his time and opportunities that he was early qualified to take a prominent position under his father. In this way he became thoroughly acquainted with all the points of interest on Lake Ontario, especially with those places where navigation was dangerous. The knowledge thus acquired, enabled him in after years not only to be of service to his father in their own business transactions, but to render efficient aid to his country in her hour of perilous need.

Five years apprenticeship with his father had made young Richardson thoroughly conversant with the topography of the lakes and rivers. The dangerous harbor entrances, the rocks, channels, and shoals belonging to these waters, were as familiar to him as the streets of his native town are to a landsman. Therefore desirous of rising in his profession, he, with his father's concurrence, in 1809, entered the Provincial Marine, being then but eighteen years of age.

About this time he suffered, in the death of his mother, the first great sorrow of his life.

This was a great bereavement to the whole family. To James it was especially so, at this critical period in his career, when, being no longer under his father's watchful care, he so much needed the counsels and admonitions of a mother. His parents had early implanted in his heart the principles of integrity and honor, and these with the natural good sense of the young man proved a safeguard against the temptations to which his position exposed him. The firmness of his principles was manifested by his subsequent conduct.

After his entrance into the Provincial Marine service, his strict obedience to orders, coupled with his excellent moral character and gentlemanly bearing, gained for him the confidence and respect of the officers and men. The estimation in which his trustworthiness and skill in lake navigation were held, was evinced upon the breaking out of the war of 1812, between the American and British governments; when he being but twenty-one, received a Lieutenant's commission in the Provincial Marine, in which capacity he served his King and country with great fidelity and efficiency.

A change was however at hand in the management of this department of the service.

With respect to this change the Bishop says :

" From some mistrust that our Provincial Marine would not be adequate to the increasing emergencies of the war, application was made to the Admiralty of England for aid from the Royal Navy. Accordingly, in the winter of 1813, Captain Barclay, accompanied by Commodores Downie and Pring, Lieutenant Scott and a few warrant officers and sailors, was despatched from Halifax across the wilderness, through storms, frosts and snowdrifts to Quebec, thence to Kingston, where they arrived in April, weather beaten, exhausted and almost 'done up.' Captain Barclay took command, till the arrival in May of Sir James L. Yeo with 500 officers and men direct from England.

" I had the honor to be despatched by Capt. Barclay, with the gunboat " Black Snake," to meet Sir James with his flotilla of unarmed Canadian batteaux and escorted him up the river, along the frontier of the enemy, to

Kingston, where with the rear division under Captain Mulcaster, we arrived unmolested in the latter part of May, 1813.

"The naval armament on the lakes now assumed a new character and position—no longer " Provincial " nor subject to the Quarter Master General, but a part and dependency of the Royal Navy. Our Provincial commissions were of no force or effect in the new relation ; yet, because of our local knowledge and experience, our services were desirable, and particularly required by our new Commander ; none however, of the commissioned officers on Lake Ontario consented to remain, except Lieutenant George Smith and myself. I told the Commodore, that if my services were of any avail they were at his command, only I would not take any rank inferior to that I held in the Provincial Marine. He remarked that the rules of the service precluded my relation as a Lieutenant among them, but he would be happy to have my services as a Master, and would rate me accordingly ; this, while it gave me rank in the " gun-room," with the commissioned officers, would be appropriate to the discharge of the twofold duty of master and pilot. In this highly responsible relation I continued to serve to the best of my ability, during the remainder of the war, and for some time after; sharing in the fatigues, dangers and exploits of the campaigns of 1813 and 1814."

Though the changes made by Sir James Yeo, in removing those officers who had previously commanded the Provincial Marine, and supplying their places with officers fresh from England, had given so great, and to some extent, *just* offence, that these officers, with the exceptions named in the foregoing extract, refused to co-operate with the Admiral, yet their annoyance at this step did not diminish their loyalty, or their attachment to the Crown, nor their desire for the ultimate triumph of the British arms. They however conceived it to be exceedingly injudicious to set aside officers who understood their men and were respected by them, and who were familiar with the waters on which they were to operate, with all the dangers to be guarded against, and all the safe harbours to be found on their shores, and who were also well acquainted with the characteristics and peculiar tactics of those with whom they were contending; while those who were to supersede them were necessarily ignorant of these things. To them the whole proceeding indicated a want of appreciation, on the part of the authorities, of the valuable services they had been rendering to the country, nor is it at all surprising that they were somewhat sensitive.

Lieutenant Richardson, though sharing the sentiments of his brother officers, was actuated by higher considerations than merely his own individual importance; he therefore, as we have seen, acceded to the request of the commodore, and continued in the service.

The campaign of 1813 opened with the unsuccessful attempt on Sackett's Harbour. As Mr. Richardson was with the fleet on this ill-starred expedition, we will give the account of it in his own words:

"The failure of the expedition against Sackett's Harbour, under the immediate command of the General-in-Chief, Sir George

Provost, which opened the campaign of 1813 is wholly inexplicable. Why were the troops not landed in the forenoon of the day of our appearance off the place, when the wind and weather and every other circumstance were favorable, with no enemy at the landing place, to oppose? Respecting this I had the honor of being consulted. The men were in the boats, the anchors ready to be dropped, the spot pointed out and reached; when instead of proceeding to land and taking the place, (which probably could have been effected without losing five lives) they were ordered to re-embark, the ships hauled to the wind, and made to stand off till midnight. Then, in the dark, at the distance of several miles, the men were put into the boats, and ordered to find their way to the same anchoring place, abreast of which they had been in the morning, the best way they could. In the meantime the enemy had posted themselves, prepared to give our brave men a warm reception; besides they had been fortifying their position in their works, and had been receiving large reinforcements, by land and water during the day. Why then, after several hours of hard fighting and great sacrifice of life and limb, the enemy driven from their works and in the act of abandoning the place, in despair had actually set fire to their own navy-yard and store-houses, a retreat was sounded, the troops ordered to re-embark, and the dead, with some of the wounded, left to the enemy, is a question which remains to this day a mystery.

I heard one of our brave colonels, as he came up the ship's side, indignantly exclaim: "Oh, if he would but give me my own regiment, I would yet land again and take the place." * * * * * * *
"In the month of July, 1813, the Americans having launched and fitted out two ships—the 'Pike' and the 'Madison,'—had them at anchor outside the point forming the entrance of Sackett's Harbour. Commodore Yeo therefore conceived the idea of a 'cut-out,' by stealing a march on them in the night with a number of armed boats manned by expert seamen, and aided by a detachment of the 100th regiment under command of

Major Hamilton, and a few marines. Accordingly, we left Kingston harbour about five o'clock p.m., expecting to reach the ships before daylight next morning, the distance being about forty miles across the inlets, and along the shore at the eastern extremity of Lake Ontario. Such, however, was the sluggishness of some of the gunboats, propelled by oars, that notwithstanding the calmness of the night, the day began to dawn as we rounded the point which opened out the ships at anchor about eight miles distant. It would not answer to approach them in open daylight, and to attempt a retreat would have been equally fatal, for they might have overhauled and blown us to atoms. No expedient therefore was left us but to hide in some nook or corner of the shore, which was then covered with a dense wood, and lie concealed if possible till the following night. Our Commodore therefore proceeded ahead to search, and found such a place about two miles up Hungry Bay to which we retired, and having laid the boats broadside to the beach of a shallow bend in the shore, we cut saplings and bushes and placed them in the water outside the boats, which were thus tolerably well screened. Our force numbered about 700 officers and men, and strict orders were given not to kindle any fire, or raise a smoke, or discharge any firearms whatever, but to keep quietly concealed in the woods till the returning darkness should favor our design. During the day boats passed, and the enemy's armed schooners continued tacking to and fro between us and the open lake but failed to discover us, which had they done, we would doubtless have had our boats destroyed and ourselves left fugitives in an enemy's land, which was covered with forest trees for several miles on either hand. We were destitute of fire-arms, for these, except a few the troops had, we were not permitted to bring, having to depend on our swords, cutlasses, boarding axes and boarding pikes for the execution of the work. In such a dilemma as that our ingenuity would have been fully tested, but happily it was not put to the trial. We escaped the notice of the enemy, but alas! not the treachery of some of our own party.

It was some time after we had made good our landing in the woods before muster roll was called, when a sergeant and a private of the hundredth were missing, search was made in the woods without avail, and it became evident that they had taken themselves off, but as there was no house within ten or twelve miles and they were strangers in the country hopes were entertained that they would not be able to betray us before night-fall. Our Commodore was evidently much exercised in mind through the day lest his enterprise should be baffled, and conversed with me, as having more local knowledge of those parts, relative to the practicability of their finding their way to some inhabitant and thus giving the alarm. Just before sundown one of the armed schooners which had been standing off and on between us and the lake, was observed to stand to the shore along which we were concealed, about a mile to the westward between us and the point round which we had come. Here, having anchored close to the shore, she sent her boat ashore and when it returned she fired an alarm gun and made sail for Sackett's

Harbour. We had no doubt the villianous deserters had shown themselves on the beach, and that she had taken them on board, which proved to be the case. The chagrin and disappointment caused by this betrayal and consequent failure of the scheme, within a few hours of what otherwise would probably have been its successful termination, may be conceived. We all felt sorely, but Commodore Yeo could scarcely contain himself.

Nothing could now be done but to seek our safe retreat. So soon as night set in, we were ordered to embark, and pulling into the offing got sight of the ships which were fully lighted up and prepared to give us a warm reception. Should we have had the audacity to make the attack, they could no doubt have sunk us as we came alongside. Orders were then given to pull for the Canadian side and make good our retreat. At day break next morning, we saw the American squadron off the point under full sail after us, but the wind was so light during the night that they did not come up."

" The following incident which occurred

during the summer of 1813, may be worthy of notice. Our Commodore in absence of something to fight, proceeded to inspect the enemy's coasts and harbours, in search of provisions and stores, which when taken would replenish us, while it despoiled them. Being informed that the United States had a large stock of flour deposited at the village of Big Sodus, about thirty miles westward of Oswego, he brought his squadron to anchor and towards evening sent in the boats with a few sailors and marines, and a detachment of about 60 of the 'Royals.' It became dark before we made the landing, and an advance of 15, of which I was one, commanded by Capt. Mulcaster, proceeded at once to the village, under the guidance of one acquainted with the place. We found the houses deserted, and not a person to be seen, but one in a tavern so drunk that we could get no information from him. After searching in vain for the inhabitants, during which strict orders were given *not to molest any furniture or articles of private property*, and while our Captain was consulting as to future proceedings, it being very dark, some one hailed us from some bushes close by. Captain Mulcaster answered 'friend,' but before the word was fully out they fired a volley which felled 5 of our 15. They then took themselves off. The detachment of the 'Royals' coming up in our rear and hearing the firing, took us for the enemy, and also discharged a few shots at us before the mistake was discovered. Capt. Wilson of the 'Royals,' who was among the 15 in advance, wore a peculiarly shaped cocked hat, which a flash of lightning just at that moment, happily for our party, revealed, and showed the officer of the detachment in the rear who we were. Thus in all probability the shape of a cocked hat saved some valuable lives. The enemy was no more seen during the night, except some stragglers who towards morning came within our lines and were arrested. On being questioned as to the firing, and where the inhabitants of the village were, they said it was the inhabitants themselves that had fired; that on the approach of the ships in the evening a consultation was held in the village, and while some would have remained quietly at home under the conviction that they would not be molested, the majority decided to arm themselves, disappear, and fire on us, some remarking that they would thus have the satisfaction of killing some of the British anyway.

This word being sent to the Commodore, he ordered the place to be burnt as a warning to all others along the coast. The prisoners being liberated they were instructed to say that wherever we came, if the inhabitants remained quiet, private property and rights would be respected; but in all cases where the people made an armed resistance and wantonly fired on us, they might expect to be punished in like manner. This was a painful occurrence. Both the occasion and its result caused me distressing feelings. How far the Commodore was justified by the rules of war, the public must judge, but that it was not a wanton and unprovoked act, as some have represented it, I am witness, inasmuch as till this word came from their own people—the said prisoners,—strict orders were given to respect private property, and even when an order was given to *burn the place, pillage was forbidden.* All we got for our visit was about 500 barrels of flour, found in a storehouse. I have since conversed with an American gentleman who was at the place at the time, and who stated that about 3,000 barrels of flour belonging to the United States were there concealed in the woods, which the darkness of the night covered from our view."

" In the spring of 1814 word having reached our Commodore, Sir James L. Yeo, that a large number of boats were at the mouth of Oswego River, laden with cannon and naval stores for the fitting out of the two frigates then being built at Sackett's Harbour; an expedition was ordered for the capture of the Fort at that place, now named ' Fort Ontario,' then known as ' Fort Oswego.' Our squadron consisting of the Prince Regent, 60 guns, Princess Charlotte, 32 guns, Wolf, 20 guns, Royal George, 20 guns, Moira, 16 guns, Melleville, 16 guns, and Netley, 12 guns, with detachments of troops from the ' Royals,' ' Glengarry Fencibles,' and other corps left

Kingston on the 4th May, and arrived off Oswego, the 5th; but owing to a heavy squall of wind they were obliged to haul off and delay the attack till next day. In the morning of the 6th orders were given the Wolf (subsequently named the Montreal,) to stand in and take a position under the fort, to cover and assist the landing of the troops. The charge of conducting her to her anchorage among the rocks and shoals that environ the entrance to that river, devolved on me. Not without some degree of diffidence did I perform the task, for not since I was a lad had I been there, and then only in small vessels with very light draft of water. I resolved however on doing my best though sensible of the weighty responsibility resting on me. I succeeded in attaining the desired position to the satisfaction of both my Captain, Stephen ·Popham, and Commodore Yeo; who were pleased to commend my conduct in their officialdespatches.

Our ship had rather a warm berth after the gunners of the Fort obtained the range, every shot telling on some part of her, a fixed object at anchor. The shots with which they complimented us were evidently hot, for they set our ship on fire three times. One of them made so free with me, as to carry off my left arm just below the shoulder, which rendered amputation at the socket joint necessary.

Our position was attained before the troops were ready to land, the other vessels keeping in the offing, so that we alone for some time had to sustain the fire from the fort. The "Melleville,' brig, and the schooner "Netley," at length came within range of the batteries, to our assistance. In the mean while, the troops with some sailors and marines having effected a landing, marched directly up the hill and scaled the fort under a galling fire from the enemy which cut down a goodly number of our brave fellows, officers and men.

Among the wounded was the gallant Captain William Mulcaster, of the "Princess Charlotte," who received a musket shot in the abdomen, from the effects of which he never recovered though he survived for several years. He was honoured with the notice and confidence of his late majesty, William IV., who placed him on his staff, as aid-de-camp at his court.

As our forces entered the fort in front, the enemy abandoned it in the rear. But although the victory was thus gallantly achieved, and the fort reduced; the object sought by the expedition was not attained. The flotilla of boats laden with the arms and stores mentioned, with the exception of one, was ten miles up the river beyond our reach, and our force was not sufficient to penetrate the country; therefore, with this one exception, and some military and other public stores which fell into our hands, nothing was gained worth the sacrifice.

The fort after being reduced and dismantled was abandoned in the evening, our troops retiring at their leisure—not "driven away with loss," as some of the American chronicles have it recorded.

There is rather a painful sequel to the history of the pursuit of this said flotilla. Our Commodore failing to find them as expected at the mouth of the Oswego river, kept on the watch and blockaded the place for several weeks, to nab them on their emerging from the river; well knowing, that unless they could gain the lake the cannon and naval stores they contained could not reach the ships at Sackett's Harbour for which they were destined; the road through that part of the state being insufficient for the transport of such heavy stores. But after the lapse of some months the vigilance of the blockade probably having relaxed, and the Americans being on the alert, they stole a march, one foggy night and morning, and got several miles down the coast before being discovered. Captains Popham and Spilsbury, with some armed boats being on the lookout, intercepted and took one of the American boats in the fog, and were informed by the prisoners taken in it, that the other American boats had entered "*Big Sandy Creek*," but they omitted to inform their captors that the boats were strongly guarded by a body of riflemen and Oneida Indians.

Captain Popham being in command, immediately, with more bravery than prudence, pushed in after them; and after ascending the creek between high banks of sand on either hand, and proceeding about ten miles, he discovered the boats, snugly moored with their precious cargoes, in a kind of basin formed by a bend in the creek. Not a soul was visible near them, and they seemed a *bon* prize. But alas! just as they were grasping them, up started from their concealment among the woods and rushes the riflemen and Indians, who opened a murderous fire on our poor fellows, cooped up like ducks in a pond. The result was the destruction or capture of the whole body, so that not one escaped to make the report. Those who survived were kept prisoners of war till the return of peace the ensuing spring.

Lieutenant Rowe, now residing near Cobourg, must be conversant with this incident in the history of our warfare on the Lakes; as he was one of the unfortunates captured. And yet, not so very unfortunate either, as regards himself, for I understand that while detained a prisoner in New England, he formed the acquaintance of the estimable lady who, as the wife of his bosom, has since shared his fortunes and sympathies, in this the country of their adoption.

I think it fortunate for me that my wound at Oswego had previously laid me up in sick quarters; for had I been fit for duty, the probability is that I would have been ordered with my captain, (Popham) on the ill-fated expedition."

The reader will have observed how briefly Mr. Richardson has noticed his own wound, notwithstanding its serious character; putting aside what he regarded as merely personal, he proceeds to give the issue of the battle. When the gallant young officer was struck, he dropped on the deck and was shortly after carried down into the sides of the ship. The remnant of his mangled arm was secured so as to prevent the sufferer from bleeding to death, and there he lay suffering while the battle raged, his ears filled with its horrid din, and his mind oppressed with anxiety as to its result, till the cheers of the victors informed him that his gallant comrades had triumphed. He had been wounded in the morning, and it was nearly evening before the surgeon could attend to him, when it was found necessary to remove the shattered stump from the socket at the shoulder joint. During the severe operation the young lieutenant evinced the utmost fortitude.

In the evening he was exceedingly weak from loss of blood, the pain of his wound, and the severity of the operation. Next day the fever was high, and for some days his life apparently hung in the balance; but at length he commenced to rally and by the blessing of God upon the skilful attention and great care that he received, he was finally fully restored.

Concerning this event the late Bishop in a letter to the writer, a few years since, remarked : " I did not fully recover from the wound till the following September, when I reported myself to Sir James Yeo as fit for service, and proposed to go out again.

He pleasantly remarked, " What ! try them again ?"

I replied, " If my services are required."

He exclaimed, " That is noble."

" He then proposed that instead of joining

my own ship the 'Wolf,' he would prefer taking me with him in the St. Lawrence—a ship of 110 guns—to aid in piloting her, inasmuch as her draft of water, 23 feet, so far exceeded that of any former vessel in the lake; it would therefore require the more caution and matured knowledge of the channels to conduct her safely. He remarked that my severe wound and consequent debility for some time yet, precluded the full discharge of my active duties in my own ship, but if I gave my services in the St. Lawrence, as he proposed, he would continue my substitute in the Wolf during the remainder of the season; and then at the close of navigation I would be at liberty through the winter to recruit my strength." Mr. Richardson was accordingly attached to the St. Lawrence He remarks:—

"She, the St. Lawrence, took the lake in October, 1814, and made two trips up and down previous to the setting in of winter without the chance of trying her prowess, with the enemy. He very prudently kept himself close in harbour, so that for the remainder of the season, which terminated the war, our proud ship and squadron had the lake wholly to themselves. Peace was proclaimed in the winter of 1815, at which event the really patriotic people of both countries rejoiced."

Some time after the close of the war, Lieutenant Richardson retired from the Navy, having decided to give up the water, and procure a home for himself in some retired place, where he hoped to spend his days in comfort. But that he should devote himself to the pursuits of a retired life, was not the purpose of the Master concerning him. He has repeatedly stated to the writer of this memoir, his own conviction that God had a work for him to do, and that therefore He had ordered his paths otherwise than he had designed, and changed the whole course of his life.

In the disbursements made by the Loyal and Patriotic Society for 1815, we have the sum of £100 allotted to Mr. James Richardson of the Midland District with the following note appended. "This gentleman was first in the Provincial Navy, and behaved well. He then became principal pilot of the Royal Fleet, and by his uncommonly good conduct gained the esteem of all the officers of the Navy. He lost his left arm at the taking of Oswego. The Society in consideration of his services requested his acceptance of £100."

He was also awarded a yearly pension of £100 sterling from the government, which he continued to receive up to the time of his decease, a period of over fifty years.

The following is a copy of the certificate given to Mr. Richardson on his retiring from the service, by Commodore Yeo:

"These are to certify, the Principal Officers and Commissioners of His Majesty's Navy, that Mr. James Richardson, late Lieutenant in His Majesty's Provincial Navy in Canada, now acting master on board His Majesty's Ship, Montreal, has served on board His Majesty's squadron on Lake Ontario under my command as a general pilot from the twenty-fourth of May to the thirty-first of December, 1813, then acting master and pilot to the date hereof, during which time he behaved with diligence, sobriety, and attention, and was always obedient to command. At the capture of Oswego on the sixth of May, 1814, whilst in the execution of his duties he received a severe wound in his left arm, which occasioned its being taken out of the socket. In addition to the loss of an arm, his general good conduct was such as merits my warmest commendation.

> *Given* under my hand, on board His Majesty's ship St. Lawrence, at Kingston, Upper Canada, this second day of March 1815.
>
> JAMES L. YEO,
> Commodore and Commander in Chief.

CHAPTER III.

His Marriage—Mrs. Richardson's ancestry—Henry Dennis—John Dennis—Their adherence to the crown—Consequent losses—Various removals—Settlement of the family in Canada—Mr. Dennis appointed to the King's dockyard, Kingston—Removal to York, etc.,—Mr. Richardson leaves the service—Removes to Presque Isle—Appointed to the customs and on the commission of the Peace—First Methodist preacher in the neighbourhood—Persuaded by Mrs. Lyons to go to hear—Conviction—Mental struggles—Conversion of himself and wife—Incidents—Their house the home of the preachers—Conversion of other relatives—Appointed steward—Called to preach—Received a Local Preacher's license—Agitation for separation from parent body.

During the war Lieutenant Richardson was married to Miss Rebecca Dennis, the daughter of Mr. John Dennis, who was for many years Master builder in the King's Dockyard at Kingston. Mrs. Richardson belonged to an old U. E. Loyalist family. Her grand-father, Mr. Henry Dennis, resided at the time of the American Revolution, on the banks of the Delaware in Buck's county Pennsylvania, where he possessed a handsome property, and owned also some valuable iron works about thirty miles from Philadelphia.

He was strongly attached to the British Government, but belonging to the Society of Friends, he declined to take up arms. His loyalty, however, led him to render such services to the King's cause as he deemed not inconsistent with the creed he held. Accordingly, he carried some dispatches for the British; and being detected, was obliged with his son John, who accompanied him, to take refuge within their lines at New York. There they resided till the death of Mr. Henry Dennis which occurred during the war, caused by apoplexy. His valuable estate was confiscated, and forever lost to his family. His son John, (the father of Mrs. Richardson,) shortly afterward joined the army.

After the termination of the war, Mr. John Dennis, who had previously married in New York, went with other U. E. Loyalists to Beaver Harbour, Nova Scotia. There the unfortunate refugees found themselves sorely straightened for lack of the absolute necessaries of life. Mr. Dennis seeing no prospect of procuring a comfortable livelihood for his family in that place, returned to New York.

Thence he went to Alexandria, in the District of Columbia, where his daughter Rebecca was born. Though he was successful in business in Alexandria, yet that did not reconcile him to the state of things he found existing there. The slavery in which the negroes were held particularly excited his disgust, and resolving not to allow himself even seemingly to be brought into complicity with that " sum of all villanies," he determined to leave. This was about the time that Governor Simcoe was inviting loyalists, then in the States, to come into Upper Canada, and having townships surveyed in which to settle them. The land which fell to the lot of Mr. Dennis was situated on the banks of the Humber, not over a mile from the site of the present village of Weston. Where the city of Toronto now stands was almost an unbroken wilderness. The family resided there for some years enduring the toils and privations incident to settlements in the wilderness.

Mr. Dennis, being a ship-builder, sometimes varied his employment by building small vessels for those who could afford such conveniences. One of these called the "Toronto," a schooner rigged Government yacht for the transport of officers and employees of the Government and others across the lake, pleased Governor Hunter so well that in 1802 he appointed Mr. Dennis master builder in the King's Dockyard at Kingston. There he continued till the summer of 1812, when he was ordered to York (now Toronto) to build a ship. When the Americans in April, 1813, took York, this vessel, then nearly completed, was by them burned upon the stocks. Mr. Dennis, as captain of a company formed of the officers and others connected with the Dockyard, assisted in defending the place though overpowered by their assailants. Mr. Dennis continued to reside in York, till his death by Asiatic cholera in 1832.

No better summary of Mrs. Richardson's character can be given than that contained in the following obituary notice of her, written by her bereaved husband.

"Died at her residence at Clover Hill, Toronto, 29th of March last, aged sixty five, REBECCA, wife of the Rev. James Richardson."

"The dear departed was the daughter of the late John and Martha Dennis, who were of the old U. E. Loyalist stock, and among the first of the settlers in the vicinity of this city, then an almost unbroken wilderness. Her father, about the year 1802, receiving the appointment of master-builder in the King's dock-yard at Kingston, removed thither. It was there, in 1809, that I first formed acquaintance with her, which in 1815 resulted in our marriage, disregarding in the ardour of our youth the privations and troubles incidental to the state of war then raging in our country, and to which, from my position in the Navy, I was peculiarly exposed."

Peace being happily restored and the country quiet, we retired from public life, and removed in the spring of 1817 to the Presque Isle Harbour, near what is now the village of Brighton, thinking there to spend in a quiet rural way the remnant of our days; but Providence ordered otherwise.

The preaching and ordinances of religion in our neighbourhood as administered by the Methodists—those earliest and most successful pioneers of religion in Canada—were, though somewhat novel and strange to us at the first, rendered effectual through grace to the conversion of our souls, and eventually to a thorough change in the course of our lives. In August 1818 we united ourselves to the Methodist Episcopal Church, and came under the pastoral care of the late Rev. Thomas Madden.

Our house now became the favoured resort of the itinerating ministers of Christ, and other wayfaring travellers in Zion, whose welcome and pious visits tended much to make the few years of our residence there some of the most agreeable of our lives. The pleasure and profit which Mrs. Richardson derived from this intercourse was evinced by the cheerfulness with which she always dispensed the hospitalities of her home."

" The impressions and calls of duty leading me forth from the quiet and comfort of this retired spot, to the privations, hardships, and labours incident to the itinerant life, especially in those earlier days of Methodism in Canada, put her faith and love to a severe test. To forego the comforts and increasing felicity of a home which seven years of joint labour and care had with the blessing of Providence provided, endeared as it was by the most hallowed associations and bonds of neighbourly regard and affection, with bright prospects in regard to the future, was a trial of no ordinary kind. To exchange these sources of enjoyment for the inconveniences and privations incident to the homeless wanderings of a Methodist preacher's life in those days when there were no parsonages existing nor funds to pay the rental thereof, was especially trying to one so proverbially fond of her children and domestic comforts, as was my late partner. Yet her piety and devotion to the cause triumphed, for when I, with much hesitation, first broached the subject to her, she meekly replied, "I will not stand in the way of your duty."

After describing their removal from their pleasant home at Presque Isle to his first circuit, and noticing some of their toils and discomforts there, Mr. Richardson adds—

"Yet all this, with what followed as we

were removed from place to place for several succeeding years, she bore with becoming resignation and christian cheerfulness. All went well till the unhappy, and as she believed uncalled for action of the conference relative to the *Union* so-called, which, with what followed in succession for a few years, shook her confidence and disturbed her mind. The remnant of the Episcopal Methodists, in these times struggling to sustain the old economy of the church, received her sympathy, but not having any society of these in the city, she was led to seek religious fellowship with the Congregational Church, then under the pastoral care of the Rev. John Roaf. With them she united, and continued a devoted and steadfast adherent to the cause of Christ in that Church till it pleased the Lord to take her to himself. In the meantime taking pleasure in entertaining the friends of Christ, of whatsoever denomination they were, and in contributing to the means for the promotion of His Kingdom among men."

"The last few years of her life were marked by severe bodily affliction, she being confined to her couch or chair, yet was cheerful and resigned. Always, when asked in regard to her spiritual state, expressing her confidence in God, and her firm reliance on the merits and faithfulness of Christ; and speaking also of the love she felt, in the midst of her severest sufferings, for God, His cause and His people."

"Her piety was not of the fitful, impulsive, or visionary kind, it was characterized by steadiness of purpose, practical endurance and persevering usefulness. The claims of the Bible, the Tract, the Missionary, and the Temperance cause, never appealed to her in vain, but each was sure to meet in her a prompt and liberal friend. Her surviving associates, remembering by-gone days, will feel that we have lost a mother in Israel."

But to return to the subject of our narrative :—Hitherto, though strictly moral, upright and conscientious, in every respect a worthy member of the community, and a model British officer, Mr. Richardson had as yet had no experimental knowledge of religion. But now removed from the exciting influences which necessarily surrounded him on board a man of war, he had more time for quiet reflection; and, just at this time he providentially became acquainted with those untiring evangelists, the Methodist preachers. The account of his conversion together with some incidents relative to his first acquaintance with several of those pioneer preachers will be best given in his own words.

"In the course of the summer of 1817," he writes, "I was led to hear the Methodists, and the first sermon I heard with attention took hold of me and was the germ of my conversion and entire change of life."

"One fine sunshiny week day in the month of July, a person on horseback passed by our house within view of the window, with saddle bags under him, when some one exclaimed, 'There goes a Methodist preacher.' 'Aye! so it is. Where is he going to preach?' 'At 'Kiah Betty's, about two miles from this on the Lake shore.' 'Indeed! Who will go and hear him?'"

"'You had better go,' exclaimed grandmother Lyons, a pious old Baptist lady, who in her anxiety to turn our attention to the things that accompany salvation, was ready to commend the ministry of the blessed gospel, though in some respects not according with her own views. Her heart yearned for our conversion to God, by which she was prompted to urge our attendance on the only means of grace within our reach."

I, with my wife and sister, Mrs. Lyons, went, and for the first time in my life I heard with effect. The sermon was founded on Rev. iii. c. 20th v. The matter of this discourse, the manner of its delivery, the solemnity and general appearance of the preacher —the late Wyatt Chamberlain, sent from the Genesee Conference of the Methodist Episcopal Church—all had their effect upon my mind. The subject was communion with Christ in the heart, attended by faith, yielding obedience to his calls. I said to myself while it carried conviction to my conscience, 'If this be christianity, alas! 1 am not a christian, for I know not this.'"

"Henceforth I searched the Scriptures to know if these things were so; but slow indeed was my progress. I was sincere in my inquiries but hesitating in my decisions. The gospel requires of us sacrifices and duties; the taking up of crosses and the endurance of self-denials; and the conflicts between the flesh and the spirit. More than a year elapsed from the time of these incipient drawings of the Spirit till I was wholly given up to God. I first saw men as trees walking, my understanding being gradually informed, and my judgment convinced, but my faith stood more in the wisdom of men than in the power of God. I knew that there was a gracious operation on my mind leading me to a new course of life, but I could not define it, nor could I say—

'My Father, God, with an unwavering tongue.'

But at length the auspicious time arrived, when I could indeed say—

'Faith lends its realizing light,
The clouds disperse, the shadows fly.'"

"God shone into my heart and I saw light in his light, 'My chains fell off, my heart was free.' This happy experience came while on my knees assembled with the people of God, at a love-feast on the eve of approaching the Lord's table. Then the blessed truth of which my mind had for a length of time been convinced, that Jesus loved me and gave himself for me, came with power to my heart, I felt the spirit of adoption and could say 'Abba Father.' This was at a quarterly-meeting and love-feast, held in a barn, at the 'four corners,' in the township of Haldimand, in the Autumn of 1818."

"As to chapel or meeting-house, in those days there was none for many miles around that section of country. Indeed I cannot call to mind the existence of such, of any denomination, in all the district of Newcastle. School-houses, barns, and private residences, offered the best accommodations that Christian assemblies could command. Nevertheless the power of God was there, and in the work of preaching and praying the ministers of the Methodist Episcopal Church, as pioneers, led the van. With this denomination of Christians I cast in my lot. They were instrumentally the means of my conversion, and I said, 'This people shall be my people, and their God my God.' From this meeting I returned home, burning

> 'To tell to sinners round,
> What a dear Saviour I had found.' "

Having given a consecutive account of the exercises of mind under which he laboured during the year succeeding the time when he first heard the Methodists and his consequent coversion, Mr. Richardson returns again to that memorable day's sermon with its results to other members of his family, and to the neighborhood at large. He says:

"On returning from the meeting that day with my wife and sister, Old Mother Lyons said, 'Well, how did you like the meeting?' I replied, 'Very much, indeed, I liked the discourse, and the appearance of the preacher, too.' Then said the pious old lady 'Did you ask him to come home with you.' 'Why no,' was the reply 'we did not think of that.' 'But,' she continued, 'would you not like to do so?' We all said yes, so her son James and I went forth to seek the man of God. We found him. He accepted our invitation and abode with us that night. Mr. Lyons then proposed to him that, as the preaching place at Mr. Betty's was remote and inconvenient, he would accommodate him with the use of his new barn during the summer, and some place more suitable when the cold weather should set in. And he stated further to the preacher that if he would establish his meetings among us, if it were but on a week-day, all his working hands, about 30 in number, should be at liberty to attend the meetings. This proposition was acceeded to and regular preaching established among us. From this small beginning mighty results have followed, for though the work was very gradual and for some time but little fruit appeared, it nevertheless progressed and matured till it took deep root in the neighborhood, and brought forth abundantly in a glorious harvest of souls."

" Thus forming an acquaintance with the Methodist ministers, and having their services regularly among us, my wife as well as myself, was eventually brought to the saving knowledge of God. We joined the Methodist Episcopal church, in 1818, under the pastoral care of the late Thomas Madden."

It will have been seen that the place of meeting had been removed from the humble and somewhat inconvenient abode of Kiah Betty, which was situated on the lake shore road leading from Brighton to Belleville, to the more commodious barn of Mr. Lyons.

But in those days it mattered little to a people hungering and thirsting after spiritual knowledge, whether the place of meeting was remote or the building conveniently arranged for worship, or not, they flocked eagerly to the place appointed for meeting, and when there listened attentively to the ministration of the earnest itinerant, and as a consequence " the word of God had free course and was glorified." Though the Methodist ministers had been sent into Canada from the New York and Genesee Conferences, yet there nevertheless existed a cordial feeling between them and the Canadian people, who gladly received them into their houses, and entertained them with the hearty hospitality peculiar to those early days in the history of the country.

Nor was this spirit of kindness confined to the vicinity of Brighton; it prevailed throughout the entire Province, until evil-minded men, who wished to destroy Methodism, assisted by others who desired to build on the foundation laid by the self-sacrifice and devotion of the American Methodists, commenced to sow the seeds of dissension in the societies. Then came sad days for both preachers and people. But of this anon.

After his conversion Mr. Richardson was no less ardent in the service of his Heavenly Father than he had formerly been in the service of his king, and he at once became a man of mark in the infant society, being in a short time appointed to the responsible offices of steward, and local preacher. With regard to the arrangement of circuits, and incidents connected with the ministrations of those times Mr. Richardson thus writes:

" 'Smith's Creek Circuit,' was the cognomen of the field of labour within the bounds of which was my residence at Presque Isle harbor. This was a two weeks circuit with one preacher—Elijah Boardman—who had an amiable wife and no children. He was a stranger from the Genesee Conference, an eccentric character but devoted to his work and acceptable in his ministrations. This circuit was a 'set off' from the western part of Hallowell circuit, and destitute of either chapel or parsonage."

"My wife and I deemed it a duty to open our house to supply the lack of both, making it both a preaching place and preacher's residence, during the conference year, without any renumeration other than that derived from the consciousness of utility to the church, the society of the preacher in the cycle of his travels, and that of his amiable wife continually. The year passed agreeably and profitably, and at the close thereof our somewhat eccentric preacher was removed to other fields beyond, so as to be never again seen in the flesh by me. Not so, however, his successor, of whom more anon."

"I had scarcely abided my six months of trial in the society, ere they thrust upon me the responsible office of Steward, the duties of which I had to ascertain the best way I could, for neither preacher nor presiding elder said a word in relation to them. The preachers in those days were very reticent in regard to finances, or means of support, somewhat culpably so, for the deficiencies of financial matters in the M. E. Church at the present day may in a great measure be traced to the indifference of our fathers in the ministerial field. Such a 'culpability,' however, smacks somewhat virtuously as springing from an absorbing love of souls."

" Three quarters of the year's labor had passed, when sitting with brother Boardman in my parlour, I enquired the amount he had received from the circuit for his labours—rather a strange question to be put by the ' *Steward*,' who ought to have known the accounts—but such, I have just stated, was my ignorance of duty. He replied " About $30." " What!" I remarked, " only $30 for yourself and wife, and three quarters of the year gone, what will you do?" He replied with the utmost sangfroid, " I'll travel as long as I can, and my old horse will carry me, and then will stop." " Well," I said, " This will not do," and bethinking me of my duty as steward I turned to the book of discipline for instruction, and soon learned my duty. Then I asked the preacher to inform me as to the respective numbers and standing of the classes. Furnished with this I took upon myself to make a dividend of the deficiency to each class; and drawing up a circular, sent it by the hands of the preacher to each. The result was a return at the last quarterly meeting of the full disciplinary allowance for himself and wife, and a trifle over."

" I specify these particulars as signs of the times and for the encouragement of others in like circumstances. But as to times; how dissimilar then from now. Then there was little if any cash in the country circuits, even wheat would bring but half a dollar per bushel, and that in barter or store pay."

" The year following, that is 1820, the Conference furnished us—Smith's Creek circuit—with a smooth round faced young preacher with a sharp black eye and firm, intelligent and self-reliant countenance, who was destined to make his mark, and leave his name in the annals of the Methodist Episcopal Church in Canada—the late lamented Bishop, Philander Smith, who thenceforth became my bosom friend and steadfast fellow laborer for nearly 50 years. He also preached in my house, and occupied in his turn, the 'little chamber on the wall.' The circuit prospered and this year the first chapel was erected a few miles north of where the town of Cobourg now stands. This was considered quite an achievement in those days, a frame building about 45 by 30 or 35. But we were a happy and united people, zealous and plain, intent only on serving God and enjoying the light of His countenance. Secure in this, the wheels Zion's chariot revolved smoothly. The blessings of God rested also on my tabernacle. In answer to prayer I had the hallowed delight of witnessing, within a short time after my late dear wife and I had given ourselves to the Lord, the conversion of my aged father and step-mother with several of his household, my sister Sarah Ann Lyons and her husband James Lyons, with such of their household as were of adult age. While yet in an unconverted state we had all come to reside there, contiguous to each other, and now, behold the change wrought by grace, one family in the Lord, walking together in the hope and comfort derived from the belief of the truth and witnessed by the Spirit. The conversion of my aged father and his wife was the more remarkable, as it was the triumph of grace over a life long prejudice against knowing our sins forgiven, more especially so in regard to the Methodists. It may not be out of place here, as an illustration of this, to record a brief conversation between him and me a week or two after I had joined the Society.

Some remarks having fallen from him bearing, as I thought, rather unfairly on a worthy Scotch Presbyterian lady, the wife of a Baptist minister then residing among us, who was about to submit to immersion and join her husband's church, no doubt from a conviction of duty, I was led to reply in a way that touched my good father, who was remarkable for his open bluntness and somewhat hasty candor, and he sharply reproached me thus :

'Ah! so you, too, must leave the Church, and join the Methodists.' I replied 'No father, I have not left the Church, I mean the Church of Christ, and as for the Church of England itself, I never thought so highly of her doctrines, nor understood them so clearly as since I have become a Methodist.'

This statement seemed to surprise him and he replied :

" Why then could you not have remained ? You might have been as religious as you please; no one would have hindered you.'

' Ah father,' I replied, that is saying but little indeed, "No one would have *hindered me."* .We *need help* to lead a religious life, all the help we can get."

" This seemed a new idea to him, and he promptly and with apparent concern, asked how is that ? Is it any better where you are gone ?"

I said " Yes ; they help me on all sides, converse, instruct, and pray with and for me."

Here, after another remark or two, our dialogue ended, and I recorded it only to show the difference between the mere *negative* and the positive in church relations. Whosoever would "work out his salvation with fear and trembling "—" Deny himself of all ungodliness, and worldly lusts and live soberly righteously and godly,"—" Take up his cross daily and follow Christ," needs help indeed, whether he be Churchman or Methodist, and if the community of the former does not furnish it he will naturally, if not of necessity, look to the latter, or some other community for it. Here is the clue to the rise, progress and success of Methodism; and should it ever fail to meet its original design, or serve the purpose of effectual help to a religious life, then God will transfer the glory to some other community. The design of a church must be answered or it ceases to be a church of *His.*"

In this connection it seems appropriate to notice the affectionate regard which the Bishop retained through life for the character and memory of the clergyman who was the religious instructor of his boyhood, which will be seen in the following extract from his manuscript, written at a late period of his own life:

Speaking of the Rev. Dr. John Stuart he says:—

"No man of his day and place was more respected by all who had the pleasure of his acquaintance. Stately and graceful in his person, dignified and yet affable in his manners, circumspect in his deportment, impressive and diligent in his ministerial duties, he maintained to the last the position of a patriarch and counsellor. A few years since I paid a passing visit to my ever dear native town, Kingston, and strolled lonely and pensive, ruminating on bygone days—my early playfellows (now tenants of the churchyard) —the scenes of my childhood and youth filled my imagination, and strongly contrasted with the altered and advanced state of things then around me. I came to "Stuart's Point," and observing the remnant of the foundation of the once venerated parsonage, a lowly frame dwelling which had once graced with its yellow front the lovely spot where it stood so many years among the lofty pines which surrounded it. I instinctively placed myself upon it, and forlorn and deserted as it was did homage there on this vestige of their home to the memory of its former pious and venerated inmates. 'The memory of the just is blessed.'"

"But to return to my narrative. After the year's labor of brother Philander Smith, the circuit was favored by the return of Elder Madden, who, by his mature experience, judicious administration and pulpit instruction, consolidated the work among us. He was succeeded by Rev. Samuel Belton, who remained two years, assisted occasionally by brothers Charles Wood, Joseph Atwood and Joseph Castle, now Dr. Castle of Philadelphia Conference, all of whom had more or less of our esteem and brotherly affection—more especially Samuel Belton, whose two year's labour was marked by signal success, in and around our immediate neighbourhood."

In 1824 the agitation begun by Rev. Henry Ryan, and those who acted with him, concerning a separation of the Methodist societies in Canada from the Church in the United States, had become so great that the entire Canadian Church was convulsed with it, and, for a time, Mr. Richardson, over whom Mr. Ryan possessed great influence, was induced to lend his sympathies and aid to the scheme. He, with other worthy local preachers, had been led to believe that Mr. Ryan had been unkindly treated by the Genesee Conference, in not having been elected a delegate to the General Conference held in May of this year (1824), and that, in addition, the American preachers, while having little or no respect for the wishes of the Canadian societies, had yet *political designs* upon these provinces. This latter supposition, which afterwards proved to be without foundation, in fact, touched the patriotism of men who, like Mr. Richardson, had risked their lives in defence of their country, and together with other misrepresentations made by designing men, roused many of the people, especially the local preachers, to a pitch of excitement not easily to be allayed.

Mr. Richardson was secretary of the Local Preachers' Conference of the Bay of Quinte District, which was held previous to the conference of 1824. He was prevailed on to assist in getting up a series of resolutions, advocating very strongly the separation of the Canadian societies from the parent body, and there is little doubt but these resolutions tended materially to accelerate the movement for an Independent Methodist Episcopal Church in Canada.

In order to allay the agitation, the Canada Conference had been set off by itself, and the first Conference was appointed to be held at Hallowell, in August of this year (1824); but those who had determined that they would not be satisfied with any concession short of complete separation, used all their energies to raise the excitement still higher, if that were possible. Mr. Ryan fortified himself with the resolutions referred to above, in order to make an impression upon the minds of such of the American brethren as might be present. Still further to influence the Conference, Mr. Ryan had advised a large number of the local preachers to be in attendance there; an advice which many followed among whom was Mr. Richardson.

Bishops George and Hedding had come in to organize the Canadian Conference, and shortly after their arrival at the seat of conference, Bishop George sent for Mr. Richardson and gave him a satisfactory explanation respecting the proceedings of both the Genesee and General Conferences, with regard to Canadian affairs.

As soon as Mr. Richardson perceived that he had been misinformed, he manifested the deep regret he felt for the part he had been induced to take, by commencing to pour oil on the troubled waters. But matters had by this time gone too far to prevent the separation, with all its subsequent train of evils.

The majority of both the preachers and people seemed anxious that the Canadian work should be set off as an independent body, in friendly relation to the parent Church, and both the Bishops deemed it wisdom to grant them their desire, as then expressed.

Mr. Richardson repeatedly stated that this action of the Conference was not forced upon them by the then Government; though it was urged on by some of the ambitious men in the church, and by the clique who sought to rule Canada, viz., the Family Compact, with other advocates of church and state connection in these colonies, who strove to compel the American preachers to labour under various disabilities.

The general deportment, pious conversation and evident disinterestedness of both the Bishops on this occasion, impressed Mr. Richardson so favourably that he ever afterwords held not only them, but the Church of which they were the honoured superintendents, in the highest respect.

Satisfied with the explanation of the Bishops, he returned home from the Hallowel Conference more warmly attached to his beloved Methodism, and more fully determined than ever to devote himself to the extension of the Master's Kingdom.

CHAPTER IV.

Former Impressions of duty intensified—Enters the itinerancy—First years under the P. E.—Incidents of arrival on first circuit—Procuring a home for family—Extent of Yonge Street circuit in 1824—How travelled—Winter of 1824-1825—Condition of the circuit—Amount received—A good colleague—Condition of the circuit at the end of the year—Admitted on trial 1825—Returned to Yonge Street with Egerton Ryerson as assistant—Pleasant colleague and prosperous year—Membership doubled—Another son—Conference of 1826—Sent to Fort George and Queenston—Admitted into full connexion at conference of 1827—Sent to the Credit mission—Labours, trials, and success of the year.

Mr. Richardson had now been for some years acting with acceptability and usefulness, as a local preacher. He had been privileged to rejoice in the conversion of beloved relatives, dear friends, and neighbours, and in the prosperity of the cause on the circuit. And while he praised God for what HE had there wrought through the preaching of the Gospel, he felt pressed in spirit to go himself and carry the same glorious message of salvation into other communities. The impressions leading in this direction which he had felt from a very early period of his Christian life, now acted upon his mind with redoubled force. In relation to this he says :—

"I now approach the event in the history of my religious life, which in its results, to me and mine, surpassed all others, except, indeed, my conversion to God. For some months, during the autumn and winter of 1823-24, my mind was impressed with the thought that it was incumbent on me to take the itinerant field, and do what I could to cultivate 'Immanuel's land.' But the thought was intrusive and painful. How could I broach it to my wife? who had co-laboured with me through seven years of privation and hard work, till we had succeeded in securing a comfortable home. Our domestic felicity increasing every year, and our future prospects becoming more promising, my income from the office of Collector of Customs increasing; my influence as a Justice of the Peace and local preacher extending; in a word every earthly tie binding me to home and its endearments."

"All this to be left behind. And for

what? Why was I called to the sacrifice? I could scarcely tell *why*. But so it was, the thought followed and troubled me." I well knew that Methodist itinerants in those days got only a very precarious support. Scarcely a parsonage, comfortable or otherwise, or any circuit awaited them. As to financial arrangements there were none worthy of the name. Anything or nothing, as it might be, was the order of the day. I knew what was before me, yet something said 'You must go.'"

"At length with considerable hesitancy, I mentioned what was on my mind to my wife. She looked serious and much impressed, but after an evident struggle of feeling, replied, "I will not stand in the way of your duty."

"That decided the matter. The die was cast. Instead of being comfortably moored with my family in this retired but pleasant spot, I must now weigh anchor, and put out on the roving voyage of life, to wander up and down, and smile at toil and pain. Well, so it has been, and so let it be, if God's cause demands it. Casting my all upon my Heavenly Father's care I committed myself and family to the toils and privations attendant on a Methodist preacher's life in those days. My confidence was not misplaced. God has taken care of me and mine all along, and I trust Him for what is to come. And now let me sing—

> ' Here I'll raise mine Ebenezer,
> Hither by thy help I've come,
> And I hope by thy good pleasure,
> Safely to arrive at home.' "

The spiritual destitution in many parts of the country was at that time very great, the labourers being so few compared with the wide extent of the field needing cultivation. The godly men whose souls were flaming with zeal for the conversion of sinners, and who were performing Herculean labours in order to present the Great Salvation to as many as possible, were yet distressed in spirit, thinking of those to whom there was none to carry the joyful sound. The Rev. Thomas Madden, then Presiding Elder on that district, who having been aware of the struggle going on for so many months in Mr. Richardson's mind, and having been anxious for the result, now hailed the decision with much satisfaction, and hastened to secure to the church the services of so promising a man.

Mr. Madden being then in want of a second preacher for the Yonge Street circuit, at that time in charge of the Rev. William H. Williams, he (Mr. Madden) proposed to Mr. Richardson not to wait till the next Annual Conference before entering the work, but to go out that year [1824] under the Presiding Elder, as Mr. Williams' assistant. The circuit was very large including the Town of York [now Toronto] and extending through eight townships, also embracing some parts of others, consequently the exegencies of the work there very much required the aid of another preacher. Mr. Richardson believing that he had been called by the Holy Ghost to the work, and having determined in the fear of God to yield to the holy calling, felt himself subject to orders and consented to the arrangement. His departure, journey, &c., we give in his own words.

"In the month of September 1824, after arranging my affairs, disposing of stock and household goods, other than what I took with me, putting a tenant into my house and a deputy into the Collector's office, preparatory to resigning it; I took leave of the endearments of home, of my dear father and other relations and friends, and embarked on board a small schooner of about 30 tons, with my dear wife and the three lovely children with which the Lord had blessed us during our sojourn at Presque Isle, besides a few things for housekeeping, and in about two days we anchored in York harbour. We landed in the night. It was dark and raining, plenty of mud, but no carriage in waiting. I went ahead to the residence of my wife's father, on the corner of King and Yonge streets. Mr. Dennis taking a lantern, immediately went forth with me. We met my wife and children trudging through the mud and rain. James Henry in his mother's arms and the little girls following as best they could, Sarah Jane minus a shoe, which had come off in the mud while crossing Wellington street. No sidewalks nor McAdamizing in those days."

Through the mercy of God, here we were, snugly quartered at last, but no parsonage, nor other house available for our residence. I had entered indeed upon the field of my future labor, but we were homeless except as sheltered for the time being by my wife's parents. Mr. Dennis having a small dilapidated house that had been once a dwelling, but was now used as a joiner's shop, generously offered the use of it rent free, while I served on the circuit, if I could so fit it up as to live in it. Seeing no alternative I went to work, assisted by my wife, and after two or three weeks hard labor, and an expenditure of about twenty dollars, succeeded in rendering the old house a tolerably comfortable dwelling for us during the two years of our stay on the Yonge street circuit."

We found the brethren and sisters in the Town very kind and ready to show all Christian courtesies, but too few in number and sufficiently burthened with their own necessities, to render much aid in sustaining the cause. We found however their hearts open, and the more so the longer we sojourned amongst them, and this went far to console my dear wife, and to reconcile her to the change of circumstances which a sense of duty had imposed upon us."

The facts here presented afford a glimpse of the trials encountered by the first itinerant preachers and their families, in this country: and which are indeed to some considerable extent, still experienced by those who are earliest in following the settlers into the remote settlements. And not a few of them have had to endure much greater hardships than any of those related by Mr. Richardson. But when we consider the temporal sacrifices made by Mr. and Mrs. Richardson in leaving a pleasant and commodious home, and a large circle of esteemed and appreciating friends; and also the resignation by Mr. R., of lucrative and honorable offices, in order to enter the Methodist ministry, we are impressed with the genuine spirit of self-devotion and love, thereby manifested by them for the cause of God, and the salvation of the people. Nor was theirs by any means an isolated instance of the spirit of self-sacrifice among those pioneer Methodists.

The reader may gain some idea of the

Bishop's first circuit, and the difficulty of travelling at that period, from the following extract :

"My field of labour, besides embracing the capital of the Province, extended up Yonge street to Lake Simcoe, about forty-five miles. Thence easterly through the townships of Markham, Scarboro, Pickering, Whitby and Darlington, to the edge of Clark, with lateral excursions to the right and left, for eight or ten miles more or less in various places. The state of the roads precluding the use of carriages, except to a very limited extent, this large circuit had to be travelled on horseback, the preacher carrying his books, writing materials, changes of linen, &c., in the historic saddle-bags."

" The first winter, that of 1824-25, was such as I have never seen either before or since. Not a day of real good sleighing on my circuit during the whole winter, but mud holes in plenty, so that the roads were almost impassable. During the months of December and January it was exceedingly hard work to reach our appointments.. And it being almost impossible to reach the town with any kind of vehicle, the citizens got scarcely any supplies from the country. The ordinary price of good firewood was but $1.50 per cord, yet a cart-load of refuse wood picked up on the commons would sell for a dollar; such was the difficulty in getting the better article to market."

"The most disheartening feature of my labours in 1824, was the demoralized condition of the circuit. It had been run over and trampled down. The class papers had been neglected, and in several places were not forthcoming at all. Complaints of immoral character abounded. Indifference to the stated means of grace was prevalent in many places; and especially so in the eastern section in the townships of Pickering, Whitby and Darlington."

"The entire amount raised for the support of the preachers in the whole range of these three townships during the year, did not exceed two dollars and twenty cents; while here our rides were longer and our labors more trying, than in the western part of the work. The whole amount of my dividend for my year's services was about $100.00 including everything. A small amount out of which to feed and clothe my family, feed my horse, and pay for house and travelling expenses. Nevertheless the Lord favoured us with health and strength and a resigned will."

What would some of our preachers and preachers wives, in these days, say to such a state of things? There is reason to believe that too many of them would be found flying off at right angles. This remark, however, is not designed either to commend, or excuse the conduct of the people to whom the bishop refers. Far from it. Such penuriousness is nearly akin to dishonesty, if it is not that very thing. It is a sin against God and His church, and should be reprobated as such by every Christian in the land.

But unfortunately for the cause of Christ there are careless ministers to be found, as well as stingy church members. It is lamentable that there are in all the denominations, those who apparently do not care for the salvation of souls, although they occupy a place in the ministry of the church. In the Methodist church there are some who pay but little attention to the class papers, or to the spirituality of the membership. The parsonage property is allowed to become dilapidated; and the general connexional interests are neglected. In fact, to judge from their conduct, it would appear that the thought they bestow upon the church seldom gets much beyond preaching pleasantly to tickle the ears of their hearers, being careful not to disturb their consciences. And yet these are the men who are constantly boring the Bishops and Presiding Elders for *good* circuits and *easy* work. Such *pastors* are always expecting the conference to give them the choice circuits, while they not only never build up circuits, but they often destroy during their stay upon a circuit what has been accomplished by other careful, laborious brethren in preceding years. Men who cannot, or will not labour to extend and strengthen the cause, should be politely requested by the people and conference to locate.

The writer recalls perplexing reminiscences of his experience when on the Stationing

Committee with Bishops Smith and Richardson, when the conference had left men on their hands with whom they could not tell what to do, consistently with their consciencious regard for the interests of the work. They would ask—"Where can we station them, that the church may receive the least damage by their stay for the year? The conference too often, in sympathy with the man, forgets the requirements of the Lord's cause."

The Bishop concludes his remarks respecting his first circuit as follows.

"My colleague Rev. William H. Williams was a thorough working man, bland and generous; unburthened with a family, he was at home wherever night overtook him. He was an excellent colleague, and applied himself vigorously to trimming up the circuit. By a judicious administration of discipline, we presented the circuit much improved, and the societies much advanced in piety and Christian life, though not in numbers."

Thus ended the first year of Mr. Richardson's ministry. It was one of toil, mental trial and small financial remuneration. But having entered the Lord's vineyard, and covenanted to devote himself to the work of the Master, he did not regard his faithfulness, or diligence as subject to the condition of his receiving an abundance of earthly things. He was contented to accept the Lord's promise, and to wait for the stipulated reward, viz: " The promise of the life that now is, and that which is to come." And most faithfully has the promise been fulfilled to our dear departed brother. Mr. Richardson continues: " At the ensuing annual Conference (1825) I was admitted on trial, and put in charge of the same Yonge Street circuit with Rev. Egerton Ryerson for an assistant, who, like myself, had this year been admitted on trial.

The circuit had this year been reduced by the separation from it of the eastern section, which enabled us to devote more time and labour to the town of York. A more agreeable and useful colleague I could not have desired. We laboured together with one heart and mind, and God was graciously pleased to crown our united efforts with success—we doubled the members in society, both in town and country, and all was harmony and love. Political questions were not rife—indeed were scarcely known among us. The church was an asylum for any who feared God and wrought righteousness, irrespective of any party whatever. We so planned our work as to be able to devote one week out of four exclusively to pastoral labour in the town, and to preach there twice every Sabbath, besides meeting all the former appointments in the townships east and west bordering on Yonge Street for 45 or 50 miles northward to Roach's Point, Lake Simcoe.

"This prosperous and agreeable state of things served to reconcile both my dear wife and myself to the itinerant life, with all the attendant privations and hardships incident to those times.

"It pleased God on the 29th of December, this year, 1825, to add another son—Robert, to my other sweet children; and a fine boy he was. And although, at the age of four and a half years, the same Divine Being who gave, saw it wise and good to remove him from us by death, nevertheless, we are fain to believe it will enhance our felicity in the eternal world of joy, to which we have every reason to believe he was thus early translated."

The Conference of 1826, was held in the township of Hamilton, about three miles north of the present site of Cobourg; and again the venerable Bishop George presided.

Rev. Nathan Bangs was also present at this Conference. He came officially, in order to interest the preachers in the circulation of the New York Christian Advocate, which he succeeded in doing. Of the preachers there assembled, there was none probably who took a deeper interest in the circulation of that paper than did Mr. Richardson. It may be remarked, *en passant*, that the paper was well received throughout the province.

Mr. Richardson was, this year, sent to labor at Fort George and Queenston. Here the societies were small, and not very well able to support their preacher. There was no parsonage, and again he had to make such provision as he could for his family. The Minutes show that he had but 36 members on which to depend for support; nevertheless both he and Mrs. Richardson went cheerfully to the work assigned them by the Conference. His labors on this circuit were circumscribed within much more narrow limits than on his preceding one; being confined to Niagara, Queenston,—" seven miles up the river and the cross roads four miles westerly.

During the year there were not more than fifty souls under his pastoral care. The amount raised on the circuit amounted to about $50.00, and a little more was added at the Conference; but with the self-sacrificing spirit of the times, Mr. Richardson made up the deficiency out of his private means, and left the unpromising field at the end of the year, having reason to hope that his year's labour had not been altogether in vain.

In 1827 the Conference was held in Hamilton, Gore District, now the city of Hamilton, Bishop Hedding presiding Here Mr. Richardson was admitted into full connection, and ordained Deacon.

The following is a copy of Mr. Richardson's "Parchment of Ordination," the large wax seal having stamped upon it the initials E. H.

"KNOW ALL MEN BY THESE PRESENTS—

THAT I, Elijah Hedding, one of the Bishops of the Methodist Episcopal Church in America, under the protection of ALMIGHTY GOD, and with a single eye to His Glory, by the imposition of my hands and prayer, have this day set apart James Richardson for the office of a DEACON in the said Methodist Episcopal Church; a man whom I judge to be well qualified for that work; and I do hereby recommend him to all whom it may concern, as a proper person to administer the ordinances of Baptism Marriage, and the Burial of the Dead, in the absence of an Elder; and to feed the flock of CHRIST, so long as his spirit and practice are such as become the Gospel.

IN TESTIMONY WHEREOF, I have hereunto set my hand and seal, this second day of September, One-thousand eight hundred and twenty-seven.

(L.S.)   ELIJAH HEDDING.
Hamilton, U. C.

By the Conference of 1827, Mr. Richardson was removed from Fort George and Niagara to the "River Credit;" his own account of the year's work on this interesting field of labor is brief, and as follows :

"My destination for the ensuing year was the River Credit, as missionary to the Chippewa Indians, there settled in log dwellings which the Government, two years previously, had erected for their accommodation; the cost being charged on the annuity paid for their lands."

"These poor Indians, numbering between one and two hundred, had been brought, by the power of Gospel truth, from the lowest degradation of fallen humanity—abandoned indeed to drunkenness and debauchery—to be virtuous, sober, and happy Christians. They were now God's poor; and though my fare among them was coarse and scanty, I spent the year with cheerfulness, and hope that my labors contributed to bringing them into the way of salvation."

"There being no house in which I could place my family, I was forced to billet them on my good father and mother-in-law in the town of York, about sixteen miles from my mission, till I could erect a parsonage. But here was a puzzle—a house to be built, but without the money to build it, except $100, furnished by the presiding elder Rev. W. Case. My first thought was to employ the Indians to cut and hew the pine timber of which there was abundance growing in the vicinity; and by means of a yoke of oxen which they possessed, it was brought to the desired spot, where under the direction of a carpenter the house was raised. But, oh! the task I had to get these children of nature out every morning, and keep them at work through several hours each day. They appeared willing and began cheerfully, but then they would fly off at a tangent, or loiter at intervals, so that winter was at hand ere my house showed itself erect, nor was it ready for the reception of my family before the middle of January. Then I moved in without a chimney or plastered walls, the partitions being of boards, and the openings between the logs chinked. Yet it was our *home* where peace and comfort predominated. To meet the expenses incurred for lumber, nails, joiner work, etc. which amounted to about $250, I had to solicit aid from the gentlemen of York, many of them outside of the Methodist fraternity, chiefly of the Church of England, who, I am happy to say for the most part responded cheerfully, if not largely—small subscriptions being in those times the order of the day.

"The Indians—especially the women—suffered severely from complaints of body, induced mostly from change in the modes and habits of living. The winter was open, and therefore very sloppy, and their moccasins of deer-skin being very porous would let in the water. The pernicious effect of this was counteracted while sleeping in their wigwams, by the fire in the centre acting on the soles of their feet, but now having resorted to bedsteads away from the fire, in imitation of civilized life, the effect of wet feet daily evinced itself in sudden attacks of inflammation of the chest, of which several died. I therefore advised them, either to return to the camp fire, or to provide themselves with strong leather boots or shoes like the white people.

The summer of 1828 was remarkable for the prevalence of bilious fever, not only amongst the Indians, but throughout the Province. Several of my flock fell under it in the month of August—the type in some cases resembling yellow fever. It was a fearful and gloomy season; yet the consolations of our holy religion in the dying hour evinced its genuineness."

All that Mr. Richardson received for his year's services—and we have seen how arduous they were—was $200, besides a salmon now and then, presented by one or other of the grateful Indians. In the autumn of this year (1828) he removed again to York with his family, where he could make them more comfortable than was possible on the mission, and awaited the action of the ensuing conference which was at hand.

CHAPTER V.

Conference of 1828—Mr. Richardson Secretary—Separation from M. E. Church in America—Sent to Niagara—Extent of the circuit—Continued second year—Colleagues—State of circuit at the end of two years—Family afflictions and bereavements—Conference of 1830—Ordination to elder's orders—Why not sooner—Bishop Hedding and the Conference—Stationed at Kingston—Colleague—Conference of 1831—Appointed P. E. of Niagara District—Quarterly meetings—Conversion of his eldest daughter—Her marriage and death—Remarkable increase in members—1816—Treaty of 1820—Conference of 1832—Causes leading to the measure then initiated—Unwillingness to consult the people—Mr. Richardson appointed Editor of Christian Guardian—State Grants for church purposes—His opposition—His evidence before the Committee of the House—Dissolves his connection with the Conference.

The Conference of 1828 was held in Switzer's chapel, Ernestown, which was at that time embraced in the Bay of Quinte circuit It commenced its session on the 2nd of October. Bishop Hedding presided over this memorable conference of which Mr. Richardson was chosen secretary. What his views were concerning the action of that conference, regarding the separation from the Methodist Episcopal Church in the United States, will be most correctly ascertained from his own words:

"At this conference the decisive step of separation from the General Conference of the M. E. Church in the United States was taken. We resolved ourselves into an independent Methodist Episcopal Church in Canada, in friendly relations towards the former body, whose General Conference had the preceding May, conceded to us the right so to do."

"This step was fraught with results, for good or ill, according as it is viewed by different parties, from their several stand points. It was deemed necessary then, by the majority, because of the political relations of the two countries, and the difficulty attendant on obtaining our legal right to hold church property, and solemnize matrimony. Others, viewing the church as Catholic, or Universal in her design and character, judged it wrong to limit her jurisdiction by national or municipal boundaries. Be this as it may, the result to Methodism, in Canada, has been the reduction, and for a time, the almost annihilation of the Methodist Episcopal Church. A state of things not contemplated at the time."

It will be seen from the above that subsequent experience led Mr. Richardson to regret that the scheme of separation had ever been agreed to. Though designed as a peace measure, he saw that instead of accomplishing the desired object, it had acted as an opening wedge which rendered possible several serious consequences to both bodies, which were not at the time contemplated as within the range of probabilities. Political issues in each country were subsequently made to hinge on this action.

In Canada. the withdrawal of the jurisdiction of the General Conference of the M. E. Church in America, was made by certain parties the pretext for disregarding the agreement of 1820; the results of which are too well known to require recapitulation here.

Political and party feeling in the United States on the subject of slavery running very high, made itself felt in the Methodist Episcopal church in that country. In 1844, the

Southern conferences of that church demanded a separation from the body, claiming their right to do so upon the precedent established in the arrangement made by the parent body with regard to the Canada Conference. Methodist history informs us how that separation was effected, and the consequences which followed. And even after this lapse of time there is still a spirit of unrest and fickleness affecting the minds and conduct of many Methodists, both in this country and in the United States, the legitimate fruit of the well meant, but mistaken legislation of this conference of 1828.

Mr. Richardson resumes: "Not having, as we judged, a man fully competent to govern us, we sought abroad for a Bishop, and our choice fell on Dr. Wilbur Fisk, of the New England Conference. The Rev. Egerton Ryerson was deputed to wait on him to obtain his acceptance of the office, but much to our regret he declined. Elder Case was made General Superintendent *pro tem.* without episcopal orders."

It may be well in this connection to state,

that about this time Dr. Bangs was also invited to become a Bishop of the Methodist Episcopal Church in Canada, but he also declined. And afterwards the Rev. J. B, Stratten, of the New York Conference, was invited to fill the office, with a similar result.

At the Conference of 1828 Mr. Richardson was appointed to the " Niagara circuit." This was not the Fort George and Niagara circuit before mentioned, but a field of labor entirely new to him, which received its name from the Niagara country. Some idea of the extent of this circuit may be formed by the following extract from Mr. Richardson's manuscript.

"It" (the circuit) " extended from the old 'Warner's chapel' on the east to the 'Fifty mile creek' in Saltfield on the west, and embraced the townships of Niagara, in part, Grantham, Clinton, Grimsby, Saltfleet, in part, Thorold, South Gainsboro, Caistor in part, and Canboro, with Dunnville on the Grand River. I made my home at St. Catharines it being head quarters. I rented a small house in the village which was then a town in embryo. On this extensive circuit

I remained and labored two years, having for colleague the first year, Joseph Gatchel, and the second, Edmund Stoney. The brethren were kind, and I formed a pretty general acquaintance and some intimate friendships. The friendship then formed with Dr. Beadle and his family, was terminated only by his death a few years since. My labors were, I trust, profitable, and the effect lasting. I left the circuit in a wholesome and prosperous state. The following years witnessed an extensive and glorious revival of the work of God. Methodism took a deep hold among the people throughout that region, and the result is strikingly visible at the present day."

Hitherto the family of Mr. Richardson had been exempt from very serious affliction or bereavement, but a change was at hand. Toward the close of his second year on this circuit his two youngest children were seized with dysentery of such a malignant type that in a short time it terminated in their death. Mr. Richardson touchingly refers to this bereavement and to the subsequent illness of other members of his family in the following extract:

"About 3 o'clock p.m. the grim "monster," entered our dwelling and seized Robert as his victim, and at 8 o'clock next morning Joseph breathed his last. They were enclosed in the same coffin, the younger one in the arms of the elder. The blow was severe, and the bereavment such, that at times I felt a difficulty in breathing, so heavy was the burden on my heart, yet believing that our Heavenly Father had some wise and gracious design I submitted to the blow and could kiss the hand that inflicted it."

"Our trials however did not terminate with the death of these children. About a week after their interment, my eldest, and now only son, James Henry, was brought low with an attack of inflammatory rheumatism, principally in his knees; for some days he lay between life and death. He however rallied and by the time we had to remove from the circuit he was able to get about by the aid of crutches. The disease also extended to my daughter Sarah Jane, and crippled her ankles and feet so that when in September I took my family to Kingston, whither the Conference of 1830 had sent me, she had to be conveyed by the boatmen from the steamer to my brother's house. Happily both survived to add to my comfort in my declining years.

The Conference of 1830 commenced its session on the 17th of August, at Kingston. Bishop Hedding had been invited to attend, that he might ordain the several candidates who had been elected to deacon's and elder's orders.

Mr. Richardson having been ordained deacon in 1827, was eligible to elder's orders at the Conference of 1829, but no " Bishop yet been elected and consecrated by the Canadian body, and there being none present from the parent body, the conference was compelled to defer the ordinations until either a Bishop from the M. E. Church in the United States could be in attendance, or one could be elected and consecrated to the episcopal office for the Methodist Episcopal Church in Canada.

So tenacious was the Conference of ordination by a Bishop duly consecrated to that office by the imposition of hands, that the ordination of several of the preachers was deferred from year to year after they had been duly elected to order, till a bishop regularly consecrated could be had to officiate it. This being while they had a General Superintendent in the person of "Elder Case." But owing to their regard for this truly Wesleyan principle, Bishop Hedding was invited to attend the Conference of 1830 and perform those ordinations. The Conference in order to express their appreciation of the fraternal feeling existing between the two bodies, as manifested by the attendance of Bishop Hedding, at this time the following resolutions were adopted. "*Resolved*, 1st. That this Conference feel highly gratified with and grateful for the visit of Bishop Hedding amongst us."

"2nd. That he is respectfully invited to take a seat in this Conference and to assist us by his counsel and advice."

"3rd. That Bishop Hedding is most respectfully requested to preside during the religious services of the next Sabbath, and to ordain those preachers who may be presented as suitable candidates for ordination."

In accordance with the foregoing, Bishop

Hedding proceeded with the ordination, Mr. Richardson being one of those ordained to elder's orders.

The following is a copy of the parchment received by him:

"KNOW ALL BY THESE PRESENTS THAT I ELIJAH HEDDING, one of the Bishops of the Methodist Episcopal Church in America, under the protection of ALMIGHTY GOD, and with a single eye to His glory, by the imposition of my hands and prayer, being assisted by the Elders present, have this day set apart James Richardson for the office of an *Elder* in the Methodist Episcopal Church in Canada, a man who, in the judgment of the Conference is well qualified for the work: and he is hereby recommended to all whom it may concern as a proper person to administer the sacraments and ordinances and to feed the flock of Christ, so long as his spirit and practice are such as become the gospel of Christ.

IN TESTIMONY WHEREOF I have hereunto set my hand and seal this twenty-second day of August, in the year of our Lord one-thousand eight-hundred and thirty.

ELIJAH HEDDING.

Kingston, U. C."

Mr. Richardson was this year stationed at Kingston. His colleague was Rev. Richard

Jones. The circuit was a large one, including besides the town, a range of adjacent country on the west as far as a place called Sutcliff's School House and Mill Creek, in Ernestown, Loughboro, and Portland, on the north, and Gananoque on the east. On this circuit their rides were long and fatiguing, owing to the distance between the appointments; during this year nothing of note occurred.

The Conference of 1831 was held in York, commencing 31st of August. Mr. Richardson was appointed Presiding Elder of the Niagara district, which necessitated his removal from Kingston. He accordingly returned to York where he rented a house, and settled his family. Having in former years been very popular as a pastor on several of the circuits embraced within his district, he was received in his new official relation with marked satisfaction.

The quarterly meetings in those times were seasons of peculiar interest and religious power.

The Saturday afternoon business meetings

on Mr. Richardson's district were well attended, as were also the Saturday evening prayer-meetings. The love-feast and administration of the Lord's Supper were generally attended by powerful awakenings and conversions.

Another very efficient means of grace in those early days was the annual "Watch Night," held on New Year's eve. When properly conducted it is still an efficient means of grace.

Mr. Richardson was well qualified for conducting such meetings, being a man, who, while thoroughly in earnest in his work, was possessed of a well balanced judgment, and prepared to check anything bordering on fanaticism. At one of these meetings in the old red church at the west end of Lundy's Lane held on the night of 31st December 1831, the people had assembled from about the "Beech Woods," "Beaver Dams," and around the Falls, besides some from other places more remote, when there was a gracious outpouring of the Spirit. "The power of God was present to heal." Mr. Richardson attended and took charge of the meeting.

He had taken his eldest daughter, Martha Ann, with him on this tour that she might revisit some of her former acquaintances in St. Catharines, and she was with him at this meeting, where, though but a child of 13, she was soundly converted, as was evinced by her subsequent walk and conversation. Her father in reference to this event remarks:

"She returned rejoicing in God her Saviour. The scene on my arrival home, has impressed itself on my memory. It was about 10 o'clock p.m., and while I was busied putting my horse in the stable, Martha had proceeded up stairs to her mother's bedrooom, who had retired. As I ascended the stairway I heard sobbing; my heart throbbed as I feared it was caused by some calamity, but happily my fears were turned into joy, on learning that the mutual sobbing resulted from happiness. The dear child, in her anxiety to let her mother know what the Lord had done for her soul, had communicated it to her; hence the tears of joy, and sympathetic burstings of heavenly feeling which none but those of heavenly birth can appreciate."

In 1834 Miss Richardson became a student in the Cazenovia Seminary in the State of New York. While there she acquitted herself to the satisfaction of both her parents and her teachers. It was here she met with Prof. W. H. Allen, a gentleman who has distinguished himself, especially at Dickenson and Girard Colleges; of the latter of which he has been for many years the honored President. The acquaintance thus formed eventuated in their marriage in the autumn of 1836, and the happy pair bade their Toronto friends farewell, Mr. Richardson accompanying his daughter to the wharf, little thinking he should see her face on earth no more. In three short years—at the early age of 20, she was suddenly removed from the embrace of her tender husband and loving friends, leaving behind her an infant eighteen months old. As soon as Mr. and Mrs. Richardson were apprised of the dangerous illness of their daughter they hastened to her. But an obstruction on the track delayed the train, and the remains of Mrs. Allen had been consigned to the tomb ere they reached Carlisle, the place of her husband's residence. The intelligence of her death reached the afflicted parents while they were yet on their journey, and the depth of their sorrow we leave to the imagination of the reader. Even in extreme old age Mr. Richardson could scarcely speak of this beloved daughter without being deeply moved.

But to return to the work of the district. The year passed pleasantly and the cause of God prospered. Indeed the church in all parts of the country had shared largely in the revival spirit, as the Conference returns abundantly prove. The increase in the connection during the year was 8,651. "The ratio here mentioned, when all the circumstances are taken into account, is probably unsurpassed in the annals of Methodism."

After speaking of the very prosperous condition of the church during the Conference year 1831, and up to 1832, Mr. Richardson remarks:

"But alas! we were approaching an event in the history of the Methodist Episcopal Church in Canada, which by the relinquishment of Episcopacy on the part of the " *Con-*

ference." (not of the *Church*) " proved nearly fatal to her existence, and was replete with results painful to contemplate. Her annihilation as the Methodist Episcopal Church, would have been complete but for the pertinacity, courage and devotion of the remnant who nobly stood forth to preserve her order and her name in the land."

" The origin of a desire to effect a transformation of Methodism in Canada may be traced to a movement in the year 1816, when the English Conference saw fit, for reasons best known to themselves, to furnish men and money for missionary operations in a country where the standard of Methodism had been unfurled for more than 25 consecutive years, and under that order of church government which Mr. Wesley had himself prepared and furnished to the societies in America. In fact, the only order of church polity he ever formed or provided for the people called Methodists in either Europe or America. These Missionaries planted themselves in the midst of the original societies, and fields of labor already formed and spiritually cultivated by the self-denying and laborious ministers of the Methodist Episcopal Church. In this manner were the seeds of discord first sown among the Methodists of Canada, and the aspect of two kinds of Methodists was first beheld by the wondering world, and the afflicted and divided societies in these Provinces; and although the mischief attendant on this state of things was much mitigated by the removal of the English missionaries to Lower Canada, with the exception of one at Kingston —retained there contrary to the Methodist treaty of 1820—the previous unity of Methodism in Canada was never fully restored."

The Conference of 1832 assembled at Hallowell, commencing its session on the 8th of August. It was at this Conference that the question of a union between the Methodist Episcopal Church and the English Conference, was discussed, the subject having been introduced at a meeting of the Missionary Board held at York some time previously.

To the general principle of union Mr. Richardson gave his assent, although he was not altogether satisfied with some of the proposed details of the plan laid before them.

Resolutions were, however, finally adopted as a basis of union between the two bodies, and an agent appointed to proceed to England to negotiate with the English Conference on the subject. The measure was hurried through without consulting the societies or ascertaining their wishes in the matter.

Mr. Richardson, Philander Smith, Franklin Medcalf and some others would have been better satisfied had the societies been consulted, but the majority decided that it was not necessary to do this until it was ascertained whether the English Conference would consent to the proposed measure. Such reasoning appeared plausible, but from what followed in 1833 it is evident that the unwillingness to consult the people at this juncture sprang from a different motive.

Mr. Alder was present at the Conference of 1832, and was also before the Mission Board at York, though not as an accredited delegate from the English Conference. His real business in Canada was to negotiate, as agent of the latter body, with the Lieutenant Governor in order to secure public funds from the revenue of the country to assist the

English Conference to extend their missions into Upper Canada, contrary to the express stipulations of the Methodist treaty of 1820.

Mr. Alder was an accomplished diplomatist, and that no objection might be made to his monetary arrangement with Sir John Colborne, it was not made public, till a more convenient season.

Mr. Richardson, Mr. Smith, and others being in ignorance of the negotiations going on between Mr. Alder and the Governor, accepted their appointments as usual, hoping that the union if consummated, would in no wise compromise the civil and religious rights of either the preachers, or the people.

At this conference (1832) Mr. Richardson was appointed editor of the *Christian Guardian*, a religious paper commenced under the direction of the Methodist Episcopal Church in Canada. The first number of this paper was issued November 21st., 1829, Rev. Egerton Ryerson being the first editor.

Mr. Richardson entered on his editorial work in the first week in September, 1832, and at once gave no uncertain sound, so far as his views were concerned, relative to the propriety of receiving state grants for church purposes, as the following extract from one of his editorials shows:

"We have long been convinced that supporting the ministry of the gospel from the public treasury is not only a misapplication of the public funds, but also a serious evil to the church. It may indeed help to keep up an appearance of prosperity in the extension, and splendour of her institutions; in the power, opulence, and even learning of her clergy; but at the same time it tends to corrupt her ministry by producing impurity in their motives, lukewarmness in their affections, indifference to their work, disregard to the opinions and feelings of their people, and consequently a neglect of duty, and relaxation of discipline: and the head being sick the heart becomes faint."

Again, in the *Guardian* of September 26th, 1832, while commenting upon the efforts which were then being made by the clergy of the Church of England to secure the Clergy Reserves for themselves, and to have their denomination made the Established Church in Canada, he remarks :

"A regard for the interests of religion itself, as well as the permanent tranquility and prosperity of the country, should prompt all concerned to make a *vigorous, timely*, and we trust, *final* effort for such a disposition of said reserves, as may forever prevent their becoming a source of contention and corruption, as well as danger to the best interests of the Province, by being either thrown open for location by actual settlers, or appropriated to the promotion of education in general, and internal improvement of the country."

"We would not be understood, from these remarks, as entertaining any hostility towards the Church of England, as such; no such thing; we would express our opinion and disapprobation of any attempt at like means of support and monopoly, if made to the church to which we belong, in more severe terms. We consider such a provision not only unnecessary, but detrimental to the best interests of the church itself."

Thus it will be seen that from the outset

of his editorial career, he was the fearless opponent of a state paid ministry, whether the funds were derived from the Clergy Reserves or from the Casual and Territorial Revenue, and that he thus through his paper became a "*guardian*" of the people's rights. How faithfully and consistently he subsequently carried out the views then so openly expressed, his actions, a few years later, abundantly proved. He was no trickster. Straightforward in everything he said, or did, he had no sympathy with the morality of any party, who while professing to be opposed to state grants for religious purposes, would nevertheless justify the reception of such grants by brethren associated with them, and consent to reap the benefit of funds so derived."

As the accredited organ of the Methodist Episcopal Church in Canada, the *Guardian* exercised considerable influence in the country. Mr. Richardson's fearless opposition to the reception of Government support to the churches, afforded very great satisfaction to a people struggling for their rights, at the same time it elicited violent opposition from the friends of church and state connection, among whom was Rev. John Barry, a missionary in the employment of the English Conference. Mr. Barry came out in defence of the reception of state grants, and a spirited controversy on the subject ensued between him and Mr. Richardson, Mr. Barry's articles being published in the *Courier*. This was the first intimation that the Canadian public had of the fact that grants were made by the Government to the Wesleyans, or accepted by them to be expended on their missions in the Province; still it was not supposed, even after the appearance of Mr. Barry's articles, that in the event of the contemplated union taking place between the two bodies, the Canada Conference would become implicated in the reception of such grants, or justified in any way in their reception on the part of the Missionaries.

In the *Guardian* of July 3rd, 1833, Mr. Richardson again gave expression to his views on this subject, while commenting on the action of the Presbyterian Synod of that year in accepting Government grants.

"So then the bait has taken—the majority of the Presbyterian Synod of Upper Canada have accepted the proffered boon from the Executive of this Province, mentioned by us a few weeks since. We had indulged some hope that this respectable body of ministers —most of them seceders from the Kirk of Scotland—were possessed of sufficient discernment of mind, and regard for themselves, their people, and the interests of this Province at large, to induce them to refuse the tender made; and we sincerely regret that they have not done so."

After arguing the case at some length Mr. Richardson continues:

"It is clear that nothing can be more dangerous to the liberties of the country, or more at variance with the principles of British freedom, than the irresponsible, and uncontrolled disposing of the public funds. Could such a thing exist in Britain? What would the Parliament *there* say to the granting of the public moneys without legislative authority? And shall that be practised in Canada which would not be tolerated in

Britain for a moment, because a direct infringement upon the Great Charter of English liberty? and tell it not in Gath, *Christian Ministers* too, receive and divide the spoil!! It is high time the people were awake to this evil—this source of fearful, incalculable evil to our country. The church and the state will alike suffer, unless this granting and appropriating of all public moneys be strictly regulated by legislative enactments."

* * * * * *

"Greatly as we deprecate the evil of an established church we would much prefer one, especially the Church of England, under proper and definite enactments, than the arbitrary and partial patronage of several. The former can never become so detrimental to the peace and happiness of the country as the latter."

The Conference of 1833 met at York on the 2nd of October.

Rev. Egerton Ryerson was elected Secretary instead of Mr. Richardson, who had discharged the duties of that responsible office since 1828, a change which was indicative of other and more serious ones which were to follow, the character of some of which Mr. Richardson had no conception.

As soon as the Conference was fairly opened the subject of union was introduced. Rev. E. Ryerson, the delegate of the M. E. Church in Canada who had been sent to negotiate with the English Conference concerning Union, had only just returned from his mission. He brought in his report, followed by a captivating speech in favor of the articles of Union, and the measure was driven through with a rush, there being no time taken for careful consideration of it, nor were the laity consulted till the work was done.

The name taken by the new body was the Wesleyan Methodist Church in British North America.

Mr. Marsden, a gentleman sent out as President by the English Conference, took his seat and presided over the new organization.

With others, Mr. Richardson consented to the proposed union, though he would have preferred that the societies had been consulted first. Knowing nothing of the schemes which had been, or were being conserted, between the Executive and his brethren in the ministry, whom he had hitherto trusted so implicitly, he thus expresses himself in the *Guardian* of Oct. 9th, 1833.

"It becomes us to observe that when the preliminary arrangements for effecting the union were under consideration, we were not without our fears for the results. Not in fear of a union with our British brethren, for this we have considered most desirable, from the first, but it appeared to us that the measures proposed and adopted to obtain it were not advisable or expedient and would ultimately fail of the desired end." Further on however, he expresses himself—as being now pleased with the result, evidently desiring the success of the movement. Honest and conscientious himself, it never occurred to his mind that men with whom he had acted so long, and in whom he reposed such confidence, were about to change their principles in relation to the propriety of receiving state grants for ministerial support, with as much readiness as they had changed their ecclesiastical polity and name. But so it was.

In process of time he had the mortification to find that he had been deceived, that the union scheme was not the unexceptionable measure he had been led to believe it was, that in fact, the civil and religious rights of the people had been as completely betrayed by some of his associates, as the expedition of Commodore Yeo had been by the traitor sergeant and his companion.

As at the beginning of the Conference, Mr. Richardson, as Secretary, had been superseded by Mr. Ryerson, so, later in the session, was he removed from the editorial management of the *Guardian.* By Mr. Richardson's fearless and determined opposition to the appropriation of the public funds of the country by the Executive and their being diverted from their legitimate use, and portions of them being distributed to favored cliques for ministerial support, he had given great offence to Mr. Barry and the party whom he served; and as it was the intention of the English Conference to accept the Government grant, and expend it in extending their Missionary work in Canada, it became necessary to remove Mr. Richardson from the control of the *Guardian*.*

Mr. Richardson was appointed to York District, and entered on his work with his usual energy. He had no sooner entered upon his labors than he found the people strongly opposed to the union, but really believing that it would result in good to the country, he strove to reconcile the societies to the action of the Conference.

But his confidence was to be rudely shaken and finally destroyed. When he learned beyond the possibility of a doubt that Mr. Marsden, President of the Conference, had received the, since famous, £900 Government grant, on behalf of the Missionary Society, and saw that the *Guardian* had changed its tactics, and was now justifying state appropriations to religious bodies, he was filled with sorrow and indignation. His first fears concerning the advisability of the formation of the union returned with ten fold force; but he was charitable and still hoped for the best.

* For historical account of the proceedings of the Conference of 1833, see History of the Methodist Episcopal Church in Canada, page 278 and following pages.

The newly appointed editor having come out with a series of articles, the celebrated "Impressions," Mr. Richardson could no longer close his eyes to the humiliating fact that the cause of civil and religious liberty had been betrayed into the hands of the Church and State party. It was now very evident to the friends of civil and religious liberty why Mr. Richardson had been removed from the editorial chair. The brave soldier, the devoted minister of Christ, who had fought and bled so nobly for his native country in early manhood, and who was now equally jealous for the honor of his Divine Master, was exceedingly grieved. For three years he worked hard to bring his brethren back to their former honorable position in relation to the "Grants," but to no purpose.

The agents of the English Conference sympathized with the "Family Compact," and these with several of the Canadian preachers were playing into the hands of the dominant party, the "Compact" through an irresponsible Executive, who was furnishing the agents of the Missionary Society in turn, with the public money in direct opposition to the House of Assembly. How this state of things created the dissatisfaction and excitement which culminated in the revolt of 1837 we leave to history; it is only necessary to refer to it here so far as it concerned Mr. Richardson, who was called before a committee of the House to give his testimony in regard to this vexed question.

So distasteful to the people were the Government grants for religious purposes that the Provincial House of Assembly, in 1836, appointed a committee to investigate the matter and report to the House.

The report, from which we have only space for a few extracts, commences as follows:

To The Honorable The Commons House of Assembly.

The Committee appointed by your Honorable House to inquire whether any money has been paid by the Government to any religious denomination in this Province, and if so, what the purposes are to which such grants—if any—have been applied; and that the said committee have authority to summon witnesses, and call for the production of papers and records, and to report from time to time by address or otherwise—BEG LEAVE TO REPORT AS FOLLOWS: That in pursuance to the order of your Honorable House your committee proceeded to the consideration of the first subject of enquiry, namely, whether any money has been paid by the Government to any religious denominations in this Province."

"Upon referring to the official returns laid before your Honorable House during the last Session of Parliament, it appears that certain sums of money have been paid from the revenue of the Province to the following denominations, viz: the Church of England, the Roman Catholic Church, the Established Church of Scotland, the United Presbyterian Synod, the British Wesleyan Conference, or the Wesleyan Methodist Society, the Canadian Wesleyan Conference."

"The fact that grants have been made and received by the above denominations is sufficiently established by the correspondence between the Secretary of his Excellency the Lieutenant Governor and the parties concerned, together with the Receiver General's account of the expenditure of the casual and territorial revenue, all of which documents are among the records of your Honorable House."

On the 4th page of the Report it is stated that—

"Whatever coloring may be given to the whole transaction, one thing is clear, that the grants of money have been made whether they were made directly to the Canada Conference, or not, and that the Conference or the Connexion have become participators therein."

This item of the Report had reference to the attempt made by prominent members of the Canada Conference to shift the odium of having received the Government grant upon the British Conference, while, at the same time the money was being expended in Canada. The committee were determined to gain all the information they could upon the subject, and hence their close questioning of the witnesses whom they summoned to appear before them. The following is Mr. Richardson's testimony on that occasion, and abundantly proves his unbending integrity. The Committee asks, Question "216."

"Will you explain to the committee the difference between receiving Government grants direct, or receiving them from that Society, or body, who received them from the Government?"

Mr. Richardson—"The difference is obvious—the one case receiving them directly, the other indirectly.'

Quest. 217.—" Is there any difference in the effects, consequences, or propriety of such proceedings?"

Mr. Richardson,—" There is little or no difference, in my opinion."

Quest. 218,—" In such a case, if there is anything so morally wrong, or injurious in a part of your conference being paid in such a manner, do you consider the whole conference implicated by not exercising the powers with which they are vested to prevent it."

Mr. Richardson—" This question calls for an expression of opinion obvious to all—that if anything be morally wrong on the part of any of the members of the conference, the whole body must be in some measure implicated, unless they exercise what powers they possess to prevent or correct it."

After the examination of other witnesses in reference to this point, Mr. Richardson, as a member of the Canada Wesleyan Conference, was again called before the committee, and examined with regard to the views of the Wesleyan laity on the question of receiving the Government Grants. The following is an extract of their questions and his replies.

Quest. 334,—" Have the Societies of the church to which you belong been troubled or agitated about the grants of money made by the Government to the Methodists ?"

Mr. Richardson—" They have I think to a considerable extent."

Quest. 335.—" Did those agitations arise from the grants themselves, or from misrepresentations respecting them ?"

Mr. Richardson—" No doubt misrepresentations respecting them have increased the agitation. Nevertheless, several of the societies within my knowledge have manifested considerable anxiety relative to those money grants after they were correctly informed of every particular respecting them. When the reports of these grants having been given, appeared, I had occasion to explain at the quarterly meeting. Those explanations relieved their minds under an expectation that as the Canada Conference had not been made acquainted with the reception of them, they would at their ensuing meeting disavow any participation in them, and declare their adherence to their former principles relative to grants from the public funds for the support of the Christian ministry. This not being done in a satisfactory manner, this agitation, to a great extent, though not as violent as at first, still continues."

Mr. Richardson's honest answers to the questions put to him by this Committee, brought down on him the serious displeasure of a very large majority of the more prominent members of the Canada Conference, who, forgetful of their former denunciations of the policy of the Executive, in making grants of public moneys to religious bodies, were now not only anxious to participate in them, but were also clamouring for a division of the Clergy Reserves among certain sects, in order that their body " might enjoy a moiety of a baneful monopoly against which they themselves had, at one time, so nobly protested."

In vain Mr. Richardson used his influence to bring the Conference back to their former position on this point; and being convinced that further effort on his part was useless, as the friends of state patronage were increasing in the Conference year by year instead of decreasing, he, in 1836, dissolved his connection with the Wesleyan body, with which he had been associated since 1833. Nor could he have remained longer, consistently with his oft repeated expressions of opposition to the reception of the Government money by religious bodies.

Although Mr. Richardson could not induce the Canada Conference to reject the Government grant, which their connection with the English Conference had caused to be offered to them, he nevertheless lived to see the day when his much loved native land was freed from the curse of a state paid ministry, and to strengthen by his influence the movement which resulted in the secularization of the Clergy Reserves.* Even in old age he would express himself very warmly on this subject, being very much interested in the progress of the bill for the disestablishment of the Irish church, and indulging the hope, in which, however, he was disappointed, that he might yet see a similar bill passed in regard to England. The patriotic christian Canadian can scarcely fail to admire the course pursued by Mr. Richardson in this matter, or indeed in the course of all the actions of his public career.

* Though Mr. Richardson was favourable to the secularization of the Clergy Reserves, he was yet very much opposed to the Commutation clause in the Act by which they were secularized.

CHAPTER VI.

Removes to State of New York—Pastor of M. E. Church in Auburn N. Y. one year.—Returns to his native land in 1837—Re-unites with the M. E. Church in Canada, and stationed in Toronto—Appointed General Missionary by the conference of 1838—Incident—Secretary of Conference of 1839—Stationed in Toronto—1840 Agent of the Bible Society by permission of the Conference—Notice of his labors in connection therewith—Tribute to his memory—Notice of his connection with the Temperance Reformation Society—In 1852 and 1853 P. E.—In 1854 Superannuated—Again on a District 1858.

Shortly after Mr. Richardson's withdrawal from the Wesleyan Conference he removed to Auburn in the State of New York, where he accepted the charge of a Methodist church. Here, however, he only remained one year, being too warmly attached to his native land to be willing to make a permanent home for himself in any other. In 1837 he returned to Toronto, earnestly desiring that "God would direct his steps and open up his Providential way." On his arrival at Toronto, after leaving the steamboat he was passing up Yonge St., when providentially he fell in with Rev. Philander Smith. The meeting though unexpected was none the less agreeable to both parties. They had been old and fast friends for years and had long been co-laborers in the Conference and church; they had both been oppressed with similar fears in 1832, in regard to the proposed changes in the polity of the Church, and had been grievously disappointed in the results which followed the action of 1833, and deeply did they regret that they had ever consented to the proposed changes, or allowed themselves to be identified with the new movement.

Then and there, they arranged for an interview. In the long and serious conversation which followed they carefully reviewed the past history of Methodism, and earnestly considered the probable future welfare of the church, and of the country. After seeking Divine guidance as to their own duty to God, and to the people of Canada, at this juncture, they decided to visit the Conference of the Methodist Episcopal Church in Canada which was then in session, about ten miles from Toronto, and to ask admission into its ranks.

This resolution they put into execution next morning.

The Conference of the Methodist Episcopal Church assembled on the 21st of June, 1837, in "Cummer's Meeting House," Yonge Street.

While the Conference was going through the routine of business, all unconscious of the pleasant surprise awaiting them, these honored men of God were on their way to make the contemplated visit. Arriving at their destination, they met a cordial reception, even before the direct object of their visit had been made known, and when their object was understood they were received again with hearty welcome. Brothers beloved they had been of old, honored and beloved they continued thenceforth to be, till they were. each in his turn, removed from the Church militant to the Church triumphant.

In 1837 Mr. Richardson was stationed at Toronto. In 1838, he was appointed to travel through a portion of the work as a general Missionary.*

* Rev. W. F. Lowe relates the following incident which occurred during the conference of 1838, held in Palermo.

" During the war of 1812 Bishop Richardson (then Lieut. in the R. N.) was sent on some office business to Toronto—then called York—to Dundas by the way of Dundas Street. He was accompanied by his wife. At the close of the first day they arrived at the home of my father-in-law, Mr. Absalom Smith, who lived in the Township of Trafalgar and requested permission to stay all night. After some hesitation their consent was given. The next morning the Lieut. had some writing to do, and as that was before the days of gold or steel pens he was under the necessity of using his pen knife to make or mend his pen, and laying the knife down on the table he went away and left it. His host laid the knife carefully away till he should return, or until he should have a suitable opportunity to give, or send it to him. Such opportunity, however, did not occur for several years, and in the meantime the incident was well nigh forgotten by both. The next time the parties met was at the Conference of 1838, held in the Trafalgar Church, which Brother Richardson attended. It so happened that Mr.

Richardson was sent to my father-in-law's to board during the session of the Conference. At first the host did not recognize in the Methodist preacher, the officer of former years, but after mature reflection he recalled the incident connected with his former visit. He got the little pen-knife (which had been carefully preserved) and presented it to his guest, who also soon recalled the circumstance of his former visit to the family of his host. They were ever after firm and warm friends."

In 1839 he was elected Secretary of the Conference, an office which was repeatedly and creditably filled by him, both before and after this period, and he was once more stationed in Toronto.

Mr. Richardson evinced a warm interest in the various associations which have for their object the spread of Scriptural and other religious knowledge, more especially the Bible and Tract Societies. The British and Foreign Bible Society having established a branch in Canada, Mr. Richardson was, in 1840, appointed its agent, he having received permission of the Conference to act in that capacity.

This office he filled, with advantage to the Society and credit to himself, for 11 years. The estimation in which he was held by his associates in both of those departments of Christian labour will probably be best learned by the following tribute to his memory, from the pen of his friend and co-laborer Rev. W. Reid.

"The late Rev. Dr. Richardson, in connection with the Upper Canada Bible Society, and the Upper Canada Religious Tract and Book Society.

Dr. Richardson, I doubt not, had taken an interest in the Bible Society from the time of its organization in 1828, for he sympathized with all movements of a religious and missionary nature. In 1839 he was appointed one of the Vice-Presidents of the Society, a position which he filled till the time of his death— 36 years.

In 1839-40 the Rev. Dr. Thomson, an agent of the Parent Society, went through the country, forming branches of the Bible Society where none previously existed, and stirring up the few which had been in existence; and with the view of carrying on the work, it was resolved by the directors of the U. C., at the recommendation of the Parent Society, to appoint a permanent travelling agent. Dr. Richardson's many peculiar qualifications pointed him out as excellently fitted for such a work; and accordingly he was appointed agent in 1840, beginning his work in June of that year. I first became acquainted with him in the autumn of 1840, when he visited Grafton, where I then was settled, for the purpose of forming a Bible Society, and from that time I saw him at least once a year, till I was removed to Toronto in 1853. In the discharge of his duties he was most diligent and persevering. The roads were often very bad, and the storms severe; but no difficulties deterred him or prevented him from keeping his appointments. His addresses were impressive and full of information; while his genial disposition, the intelligent interest which he took in every thing connected with the progress of the country, and the deep but unobtrusive piety which characterized him, gained him favour with all. In the days to which I refer, there was not as much christian intercourse among the members of different churches as there is now; political, religious, and national differences were more marked than they are now. But even then, men of all churches, and of all classes had confidence in Dr. Richardson as a truly good man. He was at the time the sole agent of the Upper Canada Bible Society, and his duties required hard work and self-denying toil. But all, with whom he had intercourse, appreciated his fidelity, and were sorry when he resigned his position.

In connection with the Upper Canada Religious Tract and Book Society, I find that he was appointed a Vice-President in 1842, and in 1851, he consented to accept the appointment of President. For nearly a quarter of a century, he filled that honourable position, and on many an occasion was his well-known form seen occupying the chair at the annual meetings, when his cheerful, and hopeful words stimulated and encouraged the friends of the cause. Until recently he was very faithful in attending the committee meetings of both societies, when he was in the city, and in him they have both lost a most faithful and sincere friend."

The following is extracted from the *Bible Society Recorder.*

" Since the matter for this number of the *Recorder* was placed in the printer's hands another of our Vice-Presidents, a Christian Canadian veteran hero has passed away from among us, regretted by all who knew him, and by none outside his own family and private circle more than by the Directors of the Upper Canada Bible Society. The Rev. Bishop Richardson, D.D., breathed his last almost at the time when the Board in their opening prayer, led by the Rev. J. M. Cameron, were commending him to God, the Father of mercies in Christ.

We cannot help mourning his loss, yet ought we not rather to " bless God's holy name for another of His servants departed this life in His faith and fear, beseeching Him to give us grace to follow his good example," especially when He has spared His beloved saint to the Church on earth so long, vouchsafed to him such an unusual share of health in "spirit, soul, and body," and honoured him so largely as an instrument in the spread of his truth.

Dr. Richardson has been a Vice-President of the U. C. Bible Society ever since 1839, and was the first Agent of this Auxiliary to the great Parent Society in England. In this capacity he laboured alone for eleven years, from 1840-1851, with that self-unsparing devotedness which was so characteristic of him to the end of his days. The great service he rendered to the Bible cause at that time cannot be estimated, for a man's influence continues in many ways long after his work ceases; but that the interest shown throughout the country in the operations of the Society is largely due to his zeal and energy cannot be doubted. As part of the result, but only as a part, we may mention that in the year ending April 30th, 1840, there were 55 Branches, the receipts were £513 16s. 8d., and the issues 2,819, whereas in the year ending March 30th, 1852 there were 104 Branches, the receipts were £1,179 9s. 5d. and the issues

13,063. To the end of his life he continued to take a warm interest in everything concerning the Society, as was shown by wishes he expressed even during his last illness. He often attended the Board meetings, and helped by his experience and wisdom to guide its actions.

It is not necessary for us to say much of the close and interesting connection of his life with the history of the country, as it has been set forth in several of the secular papers, and is well known, or ought to be well known, to every Canadian more fully than we can give it here. He was born in Kingston in January, 1791. He early took to a sailor's life as his father had before him, and during the war of 1812-14 saw much active service. He was sailing master of the *Moira*, under Captain Sampson, and afterwards of the *Montreal*, under Captain Popham. In this latter ship he was the hero of one of those plucky deeds that make men proud of such a countryman. It is quite true, he was not in command of the ship, but those who understand what the sailing master's duties are, know that though he has probably to expose himself more than any, yet of all others he must keep most cool. At the taking of Oswego, on the morning of the 6th of May, 1814, he took the *Montreal* so close in to the fort that, as the Bishop himself told the writer, Sir. James Yeo was for a time very much afraid he would get her aground. The admiration felt for him by his own captain and the commodore is clearly seen in their official despatches. Very soon after he had brought the ship to an anchor he lost his left arm by a red hot shot. But he was one of those who never say "die" while there is a shot in the locker; so we read of him in those days as we have always found him in after years, ready to do and dare more with one arm than most of us with two. In October of the same year we find him with Sir James himself in the *St. Lawrence,* the largest sailing vessel that ever floated on Lake Ontario. In this berth he remained until the end of the war.

A few years after, he was converted, and was soon called to the ministry and ordained in the Methodist Church in 1824. Dr. Scadding, in his pleasing memoranda of our sailor Bishop, speaks of this as "a curious transition, instances of which are now and then afforded in the history of individuals in every profession." We will not question the epithet "curious," for it is more than curious, it is wonderful that the ministry of the Gospel should be committed to men at all, and not to angels. But we beg to add that this seems to us a truly apostolic transition, for although all sailors are not fishermen, yet all fishermen are sailors, and though the Bishops of the present day are not Apostles, yet certainly the Apostles were Bishops. But though he became a minister and a Bishop, he never ceased to be "every inch a sailor," and was always ready and pleased when asked by the Young Men's Christian Association, to come to their help among the sailors and preach at the Bethel service, and more than once he did this under circumstances in which most of us would have claimed rest. He also took the warmest interest in the Welland Canal Mission, and was determined to let no trifle, or red tape stand in the way of the sailor's best interests being attended to by the Tract Society of which he was President. When the separation took place among the Methodists in 1836,* Dr. Richardson stuck to the Episcopal form of church government, and he was always ready to state his preference in this matter distinctly, and not always without some warmth. But he was a man of a truly Catholic spirit, and showed his love for all brethren in Christ, so that his kind genial face and his fatherly smile will be missed by members of all Evangelical Churches in Toronto and throughout the Province. Especially will this be the case at the coming anniversary of the Tract Society where he presided for so many years, and where he used to delight in claiming for the Parent Tract Society the honour of having given birth to the British and Foreign Bible Society, which he always insisted should be considered the greatest and noblest of all such associations. He was at Mr. Tyner's funeral only a short month ago, and led the prayers of the assembled friends before leaving the house. He was still looking wonderfully well

* The separation took place in 1833, and Mr. Richardson did not re-unite with the M. E. Church till 1837.

for a man of his age, although he had had a severe sickness last summer. But persevering in the discharge of his Episcopal duties during the late severe weather, he caught cold while in the County of Halton. He returned home about the end of February, but congestion of the lungs set in, and he died on the evening of Tuesday, the 9th inst., in great peace, and surrounded by his family, who have, we rest assured, not only the deep sympathy and prayers of many of God's people in their bereavement; but the tender sympathy of Him, our Great High Priest, who is not only touched with the feeling of our infirmities, but who carries our sorrows. We trust that the God of all consolation may give them abundantly of the comfort of the Holy Ghost."

At the thirty-fifth anniversary of the Upper Canada Bible Society, held in Toronto, 5th of May, 1875, Mr. Robert Baldwin, the Secretary, read the annual report, from which we take the following extract:

"The Rev. Bishop Richardson, D.D., was the first person appointed by the Society as its travelling agent, the duties of which office he discharged

for eleven years with the zeal and energy so characteristic of him, and which showed his heart was truly in the work. The Rev. Dr. Gill, the representative of the Parent Society, who visited most of our branches in 1864, says in his report:—
" In looking at the present position of the Bible Society in Upper Canada, I do feel that in former years some one must have worked hard in planting our Bible standard." The Directors are glad to know that this can be said of all our agents, and some might be mentioned as pre-eminent in the good work ; yet they feel sure that all will gladly award the first niche of honour, as well as of time, to our venerable standard-bearer who has so lately left us, esteemed by all as a Christian and a patriot, and of whom even the world will join us in saying :—

> We do not think a braver gentleman ;
> More active-valiant or more valiant-young ;
> More daring or more bold, is now alive
> To grace this latter age with noble deeds.

It has been stated that Mr. Richardson served the Bible Society as agent for 11 years, but it may be remarked, *en passant*, that in the year 1847, having been appointed Presiding Elder of the Toronto District, he resigned the agency for that year and carried out the appointment of the conference. But being requested by the officers of the Society to resume the agency, he was again permitted by the conference to do so, and continued to work as earnestly as ever in that capacity till the Spring of 1852.

Bishop Richardson's zealous and untiring efforts in the advancement of the Temperance cause have been elsewhere alluded to, in evidence thereof the following is presented from the pen of Mr. Alexander Christie, of Toronto.

The temperance movement received the active support of earnest Christian men in Toronto at an early period.

In the days when "total abstinence from distilled spirits, and moderation in the use of fermented liquors," was the instrument with which good men battled the desolating plague of intemperance; the cause was advocated by ministers and others in this city, amongst whom and foremost, were the Revds. J. Richardson, J. Harris, and E. Ryerson, assisted by Marshall, Spring, Bidwell, James Leslie, Jesse Ketchum, and others, faithful men, whose very names have passed into oblivion.

But the Spoiler was not to be conquered by such a weapon. Of these early efforts no record remains, they were promotive of good, but the Society ceased to exist; "and the friends of virtue and order had the mortification of witnessing the rapid strides of the demon of Intemperance through the length and breadth of our city, marking his track with a fearfully increasing amount of pauperism, crime, and wretchedness, without any promising means of arresting his progress, or staying his hand." From 1836 to 1839 little or nothing was done in Toronto. About that time, philanthropists in other countries, especially in the United States, were becoming convinced that nothing short of entire total abstinence from all intoxicating drinks would effectually arrest and remove the destroying evil: but many prominent temperance men were slow to arrive at this conviction; in some societies both pledges were presented, each finding its advocates; and the people were free to choose the one or the other, as seemed to them most expedient.

While the wisdom of such a course may

now be doubted, let it be remembered that much obscurity prevailed then as to the true nature and effects of alcohol. Several conferences were held in which the late Bishop Richardson took part, together with Mr. Harris, and Mr. (now Dr.) Ryerson, and the late Rev. John Roaf, then recently arrived from England. The political persecutions of 1837 had removed Mr. Bidwell from Canada, but Jesse Ketchum and others heartily joined in the new movement. At these preliminary meetings the battle of the pledges was carried on with some spirit; ultimately, however, the friends in council agreed to adopt the total abstinence pledge, alone; " and at length a meeting was called, between the fluctuations of hope and despondency, and on the 13th of March, 1839, The TORONTO TEMPERANCE REFORMATION SOCIETY was organized; and commenced operations with the small number of sixty-six members; which gradually and steadily increased." From that time forth, for many years, the Bishop, with his characteristic devotion to serve the Lord in this sphere of usefulness, continued his advocacy of total abstinence, diligently attending the Committee meetings and the public meetings of the society in which we held the offices of President or Vice-President. The Society's success was most encouraging ; at its first annual meeting, in 1840, the Committee were able to report a membership, resident in the city, of 357. On the 13th of March, 1840, a Temperance Soiree was held in the M. E. Church, on Richmond-street, west of Yonge, of which Mr. Richardson was then pastor. As this was, probably, the first temperance tea-meeting held in Canada, something may be said of it here, in this connection. Mr. Richardson's good lady and family with friends of other churches, entered heartily into all the arrangements ; his eldest daughter presided at the piano, assisting a choir that had been formed. Several new temperance songs, written for the occasion, were sung to favourite airs, and some of the best known church tunes ; the association of the latter with most empathic, outspoken temperance sentiments, rather shocked the sensibilities of some of the good people—who declared they could never sing them in church without thinking of the songs with which they were, for the evening, allied; but this was a mistake, because in the experience of many of them, in the house of God, in public worship, surrounded by hallowing influences, the Portuguese Hymn and others of the selection were as solemn and elevating as ever they had been before. During the five and thirty years which have intervened, temperance tea-meetings and entertainments have become familiar enough, but few attending one now-a-days can realize the pleasurable excitement and thrilling enjoyment that prevailed on that first occasion. The Society was incorporated August 31st, in the year 1851, and continues its useful labours until the present day.

To the close of his long, useful, and honoured life, Bishop Richardson continued steadfast in his allegiance to the temperance reformation; and so much did he desire to promote it by all means if he might but save some, in conversation with a friend a few years ago, he asked if he remembered the *old* society, whose members were pledged to abstain from the use of spirituous liquors, and use wine and beer in moderation, and being answered in the affirmative, the bishop said—it looked foolish to us now for a Temperance Society to adopt such a pledge, but if a similar society were formed to-morrow, he would bid it God-speed, and every effort, great or small, to put down intemperance.

Notwithstanding, the doctor always practiced and advocated total abstinence from all that can intoxicate, as the true basis that should underlie all temperance effort ; and while now more highly organized Orders and Leagues have largely taken the place of the Temperance Reformation Societies which formerly did battle with the drinking customs of the community, in the opinion of many, these open Societies, with their open meetings, and simple pledge, have done very much to form and spread a public temperance sentiment, up even to the point of a total prohibition of the liquor traffic ; in the happy results of which labours the workers of the present day have entered, without it may be their having any knowledge of, or ever bestowing a thought on, the men who laid the foundations broad and deep, on which they are now building.

At the Conference of 1852, Mr. Richardson was again appointed Presiding Elder, a position whch he occupied for two years.

In 1854, his health being considerably impaired, he was granted a superannuated relation which he held till the Conference of 1858, when he reported himself able to resume regular work, and accordingly he was again appointed to the charge of a district.

He was serving the church in this relation when elected to the episcopal chair.

CHAPTER VII.

Elected to the episcopal office in 1858—Illness at Ingersoll and Buffalo—Cordiality of General Conference in the U. S. -Degree of D.D.—Restoration to health—His sympathy with the Government of the United States in its struggle with the slave power—Incident—Fenian raid.

The General Conference of 1858 was held in St. Davids—a pleasant little village within a few miles of Niagara Falls.

For some time previous to this, the opinion had been gaining ground that it would be expedient to have another General Superintendent associated with the venerable Bishop Smith in the performance of the arduous duties of the Episcopal office, especially so as Bishop Reynolds had died in the interim between 1854 and 1858.

As soon as it was decided to elect another bishop, Mr. Richardson was solicited by several of the more influential members of the conference to allow his name to be used as a candidate for the office, and after considerable persuasion, on the part of his brethren, he consented.

Having been duly elected, he was on Sunday, August 22nd, 1858, consecrated to the office of Bishop in the M. E. Church, in Canada, by ordination, at the hands of Bishop Smith, assisted by several of the elders.

That the choice of the General Conference was a judicious one, subsequent years abundantly proved. The friendly feeling which had previously existed between Bishop Smith and Mr. Richardson, was not only not diminished by Mr. Richardson's election to Episcopal orders, but—if such a thing were possible—seemed to be increased thereby. The Administrative ability of Mr. Richardson was very highly estimated by his senior in office, between whom and himself the fullest concord existed till death terminated their association here.

Bishop Richardson, though having a profound respect for all evangelical churches, was, nevertheless, warmly attached to Methodist Episcopacy as established by Mr. Wesley, and, like the Great Founder of

Methodism, preferred that to any other form of church government.*

During the two years succeeding Bishop Richardson's appointment to the episcopal chair he was in a feeble state of health, and his friends began to fear that his useful life might be prematurely terminated. This was especially the case in the spring of 1860. While attending the Niagara Annual Conference, held that year in Ingersoll, during one of the sessions he was seized with one of those sudden attacks of illness which so much alarmed his friends. He became dizzy, and fancied the church was turning over, and that the people in the body of the house were being precipitated into that part of the building where Bishop Smith and he were seated, and uttering the exclamation oh! he would have fallen to the floor had not one of the ministers, near him at the time, supported him.

* Bishop Richardson repeatedly stated to the author of this memoir, both before and after his election to the episcopocal office, that he had *always* deeply regretted having consented to the changes in relation to church government, proposed by the Canada Conference in 1832, and adopted by them in 1833; as the more fully he examined the history of the Primitive church, and compared it with the New Testament Scriptures, the more fully he was impressed with the correctness of the system of church government prepared by Mr. Wesley for the "people called Methodists."

He was urged to retire from the Conference room but refused, saying, "I will be better soon."

The unfavourable symptoms, however, continued, and the writer accompanied him to Toronto to consult his son Dr. Richardson as to his condition, and also to ascertain whether the Doctor considered it safe for him to attend the American General Conference, which was to commence its session in Buffalo on the 1st of May, 1860, at which he wished very much to be present.

The Doctor, embracing an opportunity when his father was not present, explained to the writer his condition, stating that the Bishop was predisposed to apoplexy, and that though he might live many years, yet he was liable to drop dead any moment. "But" continued the Doctor "he is as safe in your hands as in mine." He has decided to go to Buffalo with you, and if I should direct otherwise, it would be a great disappointment to him. I will prepare some medicine, please see that he takes it according to directions, and do not leave him alone."

It having thus been decided that the Bishop's health would be no more likely to be endangered by his attendance at the General Conference, than it would be by his remaining at home, he set out for Buffalo accompanied by the author, who had the honor to be one of the delegates of the General Conference of the Methodist Episcopal Church in Canada, sent to bear fraternal greetings to the General Conference of the parent body. The Bishop and his companion having been introduced to the Conference, were kindly welcomed by their American brethren, and soon found themselves at home. The Bishop's speech on his introduction to the Conference was excellent, though short. He enjoyed himself during the day, spending a great part of the time in conversation with his brother Bishops and other leading members of the General Conference, upon all of whom his genial spirit and dignified manner made a most favourable impression. A few days were spent in pleasant and profitable intercourse with his brethren, when he was again, while engaged in conversation with

Bishop Simpson, suddenly attacked with a spasm similar to the one from which he had suffered at Ingersoll. So sudden and severe was the attack, that but for the timely assistance of Bishop Simpson and one of the reporters, he would have fallen on the platform. In consequence of this attack the Bishop deemed it best to return home at once, which he did, greatly to his own disappointment, and the regret of the deputation from his own church, as well as that of those whom he had visited.

Brief as had been the Bishop's stay at the American General Conference, he had made so favorable an impression upon the minds of the leading men of the church, that it was decided among them to have the degree of Doctor of Divinity conferred upon him—a project of which the Bishop had not the slightest knowledge until the thing was accomplished.

After the Bishop's return from Buffalo, he took a few months rest from active labor, and by this means, taken in connection with the careful attention he received from his family he was providentially restored to his accustomed health, and permitted to serve the church as formerly, apparently with renewed vigor.

As a philanthropist, Bishop Richardson had always taken a lively interest in the controversy going on in the United States between the North and South, relative to the question of "Slavery."

At the General Conference of 1860, short as was his stay, he was pained to observe that the clouds of the approaching terrible struggle between the contending parties, which were darkening the political horizon, were also casting their black shadows upon the Conference.

On the one side were those who took the noble stand that it was a sin against God, and an outrage upon humanity, to hold human beings in bondage; while, on the other side, a majority of the delegates from the "border" Conferences were very much averse to having the "peculiar institution" interfered with. It was evident to his mind that the bitter spirit manifested in the controversy on the "Slavery question," in the church, was but an indication of the much more bitter spirit pervading the entire nation; and, with other good men, he looked forward to the approaching Presidential election with forebodings as to the future of the Republic. Though thoroughly British in all his interests and attachments, he was yet too liberal and cosmopolitan in his views to desire the dismemberment of the great American nation. Frequently, while the war-cloud hung so heavily over the United States, he would ask, "Will Lincoln be equal to the task before him?" So far did he carry his sympathy with the neighboring country at this time, that it was a common practice for him in his public ministrations, after the usual prayers for the Queen, Royal Family and Imperial and Colonial Authorities, to offer up further petitions for President Lincoln and his Cabinet, that they might be directed aright in these perilous times.

Before the disastrous American Rebellion was over, the General Conference of the Methodist Episcopal Church in the United States met again, in the city of Philadelphia, in May, 1864. Bishop Richardson was again an honored visitor. Some of the most sanguinary battles of that dreadful war were fought while this Conference was in session, and the national feeling was raised to the highest pitch of painful anxiety. An incident which occurred at this Conference may not be out of place, illustrating, as it does, the frenzy of excitement into which the public mind had been wrought.

During the progress of the "Battles of the Wilderness," the excitement was painfully intense in the Conference room, as well as elsewhere; and here Bishop Richardson had the opportunity of forming an impartial opinion of the administrative ability of the American Bishops in that trying time; especially of the cool deliberation of Bishop Ames. On one of the days of the battles, the church was, as usual, filled with the delegates and spectators, Bishop Ames presiding. Bishops Scott, Morris, Simpson, Baker and Richardson, together with the representatives from the various Methodist bodies in England, Ireland and Canada, were on the platform with him, and all the officials in their proper places; the hour for adjournment had nearly arrived, and everything was progressing as usual, when a messenger was seen to approach Rev. G. Moody, an ex-officer in the Northern army, and hand him a telegram. Immediately, acting under the impulse of the excitement under which all were laboring, he sprang to his feet, and with the voice of a Boanerges thrilling the whole audience, exclaimed: " Mr. President, I have this moment received a telegraphic despatch. General Lee has surrendered. Grant has taken the whole Southern army! Let us sing, ' Praise God from whom all blessings flow.' "

The announcement came upon the audience like an electric shock; hundreds leaped from their seats in wild excitement, but Bishop Ames was on his feet as quickly as they. With a tone and volume of voice that both demanded and secured instant attention, he exclaimed: "Brethren, I should like to see men who, in the time of such an excitement, are able to stand steady in their boots. It is not likely that such a telegram is true. We will make no such demonstration at present. What reason have you, Brother Moody, to believe such a telegram to be correct?"

Mr. Moody, who had cooled down perceptibly during the Bishop's speech, replied: "Well, Bishop, if it is not true, thank God it will be soon." "It will be time enough then," said the Bishop, " to sing a triumphant song." And as coolly as if no interruption had occurred, he proceeded with the business of the Conference till the regular time for adjournment. As the Bishop had thought, the telegram proved to be a *canard*, and our impulsive Brother Moody had to wait almost a year for the surrender of Lee's army.

After having made a very pleasant and profitable visit, Bishop Richardson left the seat of the General Conference and proceeded to Washington, then a great centre of attraction from a military point of view; and after an agreeable stay in that city, and after visiting other points of interest, returned home.

Though by no means an advocate of war, Bishop Richardson was yet far from being an advocate of "peace at any price." If hostilities were pressed upon him, he would meet force by force. If the individual subject or citizen would persist in wrong-doing, he firmly believed in empowering the civil magistrate with authority to enforce justice. Though no advocate of tyrannical or oppressive government, and no believer in the "Divine right of kings," he was, nevertheless, a decided advocate of submission to constitutional authority.

The irruption of the Fenians into Canada roused all the old soldier in the Bishop. The Bay of Quinte Annual Conference was in session at Napanee, when a telegram arrived announcing the startling fact that the Fenians had crossed the Niagara river, and were marching on Ridgeway. As soon as the contents of the telegram were made known to the Conference, an adjournment took place, in order to consider what was best to do in such a crisis. The patriotic Bishop, flushed with a righteous indignation, at once expressed his willingness "to risk his right arm, or his life, in order to repulse the foe and drive him from the Province." And had the necessity arisen, he would have entered the field against the invaders as conscientiously as he would have entered a pulpit, or presided over a Conference. Loyalty to God and his country, uprightness and integrity in his dealings with his fellow-men, and civil and religious liberty for all, were leading articles in his creed.

CHAPTER VIII.

> Albert College—Cause of financial embarrassments—The Bishop's Journey to Europe in its behalf—Incidents of the voyage—Renewal of old Friendships—Pleasant Associations—Addresses a meeting at Darlington in behalf of the freed Negroes—Aid for the object of Mission from some Friends—Speaks in Exeter Hall—Excursion to the Isle of Wight—Visits places of interest in England and Scotland—Illness—Restoration—Visits Ireland —Return home—Always the friend of liberal education—The Canadian Historical Society—The York Pioneers.

Albert College (known at first as Belleville Seminary) had been commenced at the time when the whole money market was in an unnatural state of inflation, and the contracts for building, furnishing, &c., were let, when prices in every department of labour ruled high. Before it was finished, and fairly in working order, the great financial panic came, bringing ruin to thousands, and it was found impossible to collect a very large amount of the subscriptions on the College Books. The ruin throughout the country was too universal to render practicable an attempt to raise any considerable amount by new subscriptions, and the College Board found itself hampered by a very heavy debt. In the embarrassments arising out of this emergency, and hoping in this way to obtain relief, Bishop Richardson, who had taken a warm interest in the College from its very beginning, was, in 1865, requested by the College authorities to visit England, and solicit aid for that institution. After some hesitation he consented, and in this, as in every other interest entrusted to him, he used every effort which he consistently could to accomplish the object of his mission. He was well received by the ministers of the Reformed Methodist Church, but found that both he and the church at home had been misled, by the representation that large amounts would, in all probability, be contributed by the people of this denomination for the work of education in Canada. They had as much as they could well do to support the institutions of their own church, without rendering aid to strangers. Several benevolent individuals, however, contributed small amounts, so that the Bishop's visit was not altogether fruitless, financially.

The following brief account of his voyage

to, and stay in England, we have been enabled to compile from accounts of the journey, kindly furnished by the Bishop's daughter, Mrs. Brett, of Toronto, who accompanied her father, and also from the Rev. E. Woodcock, of the Bay of Quinte Conference.

The venerable Bishop left Toronto on the 2nd of February, 1865, by the Inman Steamship, Glasgow. It being a winter passage and consequently somewhat rough, there was considerable sea-sickness experienced by the passengers, but the Bishop being an old sailor, was happily exempt from the inconvenience arising from this dread of all voyagers.

So soon as a suitable opportunity occurred after the voyage had begun, he spoke to the Captain, who appears to have been an excellent person, and requested the privilege of daily reading the Scriptures to, and praying with, such of the passengers and crew as might see fit to be present at such devotional exercises. The Captain readily consented, and the Bishop entered on his work with good effect. It will be remembered by those who were acquainted with this eminent servant of God, that he had an interesting method of commenting on the Scripture lesson for the day, as he read it, whether he was engaged in family worship, or pulpit exercises; and it is not, therefore, surprising that these services on shipboard were seasons of profit, to those who attended them. He also preached by invitation of the Captain, on the Sabbath. Thus on the sea, as well as on the land, he gladly proclaimed the tidings of salvation to those by whom he was surrounded. Nor was the favorable impression made upon the mind of the Captain evanescent, for about a year after this voyage he (the Captain) in conversation with two laymen of the M. E. Church, Messrs. Wm. Bow, and Chas. Lane, who were going out to England in his ship, informed them that he considered "Bishop Richardson one of the finest gentlemen who had ever sailed in his vessel." The other incidents on board the ship were such as commonly occur during a tedious winter voyage.

The vessel reached Liverpool on Sabbath morning, the 19th February, and in the evening of that day the Bishop had the pleasure of again engaging in worship with a public congregation on land, attending the service in the New Connexion Methodist Chapel on Hotham St. The day following he left Liverpool, and having made a short stay at Wigan he proceeded to Hanley (Staffordshire Potteries). Here he visited his old friend Rev. Dr. Crofts with whom he had formed an acquaintance some years previously, in Canada. The Bishop took counsel with Dr. Crofts, concerning the formation of plans for the furtherance of the object of his mission, and prolonged his stay in Hanley two or three days, being entertained by a kind Christian family named Martin. Mrs. Brett, meanwhile, was entertained by her friend Mrs. Crofts, with whom she remained for some weeks. This pleasant visit over, he proceeded to Manchester, Leeds, Sheffield and other cities, to deliver the introductory letters of which he was the bearer. The letters were intended to advance the interests of the College, but in none of these cities did the Bishop meet with the measure of success which he had been led to expect.

While in Leeds, a friend informed him of a meeting to be held in Darlington, to aid the freed Negroes. He had taken a deep interest in the unfortunate slaves during the years of their cruel bondage, and felt no diminution of that interest in their condition now that they had been declared free; therefore he took the opportunity of attending the meeting. He was invited to address the audience, and says: "I had much pleasure in informing the friends of the poor fugitives of the great aid and sympathy which was shown to them on their arrival in Canada, and in narrating many incidents of much interest, relative to their peculiar characteristics. As the meeting was principally under the auspices of the Society of Friends, I received much kindness from them personally, as well as aid for the mission with which I was more intimately connected."

At Nottingham an incident occurred which quite encouraged him. He had been invited to attend a tea-meeting at this place, held by the New Connexion Methodists, and while enjoying himself there, a worthy gentleman, to whom he had been previously introduced, came to him and said that he had been so much pleased with his prayer at Hanover chapel, that he would give him £5 sterling towards the Canadian work. After some time spent in the cities before mentioned, he returned to Hanley, where, upon Easter Monday, he had the pleasure of speaking at a temperance meeting, which was held in a school-house connected with the Established Church. The incumbent of this church was an excellent evangelical clergyman, and treated the Bishop with marked attention and kindness.

On the 19th of April the Bishop left Hanley for London, visiting Birmingham on the way, accompanied by Mrs. Brett. He arrived in the capital on the 21st, and took lodgings for himself in the heart of the city, that he might the more advantageously prosecute his work; his daughter was kindly entertained by Rev. Dr. Cooke and his amiable wife.

Referring to his stay in London, Bishop Richardson writes: "I would here express the gratitude I feel for the kindness and aid

I received from Dr. Cooke, and many other of the Methodist New Connexion ministers and laymen; also for the marked friendship and help given by many ministers and laymen of the United Free Methodist Church. Whenever it was practicable, I felt much pleasure in taking part in any of their public meetings, and in preaching for them when invited to do so."

The Bishop remained about three weeks in London, during part of which time the celebrated May Meetings were in progress. Several of these interesting gatherings he attended, and spoke in Exeter Hall again on behalf of the much abused African. He visited most of the places of interest in London, and then, wearied in mind and body, was glad to leave for Cambridge to visit a friend, Mr. Johnson, who received him with kind hospitality, and gladly showed himself and companion everything of interest in that quaint old town. From Cambridge he returned to London for a few days, and thence Mrs. Brett and he continued their journey to Sussex, to enjoy the hospitality of some friends who were expecting them. After several days of rest spent in this beautiful part of merry England, they took the South Eastern Railway for Southampton, to visit some old Toronto friends, who were delighted once more to meet their former acquaintances and recall the pleasant reminiscences of other years, or enquire concerning the present state of affairs in that city.

Both the Bishop and his daughter were particularly delighted with an excursion to the Isle of Wight, taken in company with these valued friends. The day was most pleasant; the scenery such as would tempt an artist or a poet into lingering longer than prudence would dictate; and the various objects visited were of the most interesting character.

They returned to London by the South Western Railway, which afforded them the opportunity of seeing more of the country.

From London the Bishop proceeded to Newcastle-on-Tyne, in order to be present at the Methodist New Connexion Conference, which he had been invited to attend. Here, by invitation, he occupied a seat in the Conference, and enjoyed very pleasant intercourse with some of the preachers, who had been old friends. Three days were spent very happily and profitably at the seat of Conference, and then our travellers proceeded to Scotland. They made a short stay in Edinburgh, visiting the various places of historic or romantic interest there.

At Farres they were hospitably entertained by some relatives of Mrs. Dr. Richardson, with whom they visited many of those beautiful glens which abound in that part of the country. Mountain, glen and glade contributed to render the scenery delightful, especially as it was now sunny summer weather; but even there unmixed pleasure was not to be enjoyed. While on one of these pleasant excursions, the Bishop became so ill that he was obliged to return to the house of his friend, whose son, Dr. Silander, prescribed for him with such beneficial effect, that, coupled with Mrs. Silander's good nursing, he was soon convalescent. As soon as he was sufficiently recovered, he set out on his return to England, taking Glasgow on the route. Here he made a short stay, and, like all tourists, was enchanted with the scenery along the Clyde. His stay in Britain was now drawing near its termination. From Glasgow he proceeded to Liverpool, and from Liverpool once more to Hanley, to spend a few last days with his friends there. He preached for Dr. Crofts in Bethesda chapel, and again spent some time with his kind friends the Martins. At Hanley he met with Rev. T. Allin, the author of several religious works. Mr. Allin, until the infirmities of old age came upon him, had been a very useful minister of the Methodist New Connexion Church. At the time of the Bishop's visit he was 81, and very feeble; but he was quite cheerful, confident and happy, " waiting his dismissal from the body." As this aged servant of God made his home at Mr. Martin's, the Bishop had the pleasure of enjoying profitable conversation with him.

The Bishop's health continued poor, and before embarking for home he consulted Dr. Ireland, of Kirkham, by whose skill and care he was again enabled to resume his journey. From Kirkham he proceeded once more to

Wigan, to visit Rev. Mr. Roaf, who had been pastor of a Congregational church there for 34 years, and who was much beloved by his people. The Bishop preached in Mr. Roaf's church, and spent several days with him in visiting places of interest in the vicinity. Thence he took train for Liverpool, and proceeded to Dublin, where he visited the Exhibition. He made but a short stay in the Irish capital, and in the latter part of July took passage, with his daughter, on board the *Cambria* for home, where he arrived on the 1st of August, after an absence of about six months. He was sadly disappointed that he had not been more successful in the object for which he had undertaken his wearisome voyage, but he did not allow his interest in the institution to flag.

From the commencement of his public career he was a decided advocate of a liberal education, and threw himself heartily into the work of advancing the interests of the Upper Canada Academy (now Victoria College), when that institution was first started. In him Albert College found a warm friend and influential supporter. For several of the later years of his life, he was one of the most highly honored of the Senators of our University, and no one was more eminently fitted for the position. He delighted in the mental, moral and religious advancement of the young people of Canada, manifesting a deep interest in everything tending to that object, from the infant class in the Sunday school to the graduating class in the University.

But much as the Bishop loved his own church and her institutions, and warm an interest as he took in other purely religious and temperance societies, he did not confine himself to exclusive association with them. Other societies and associations, designed for the advancement of objects he deemed worthy, had his countenance and sympathy.

Patriotic through his whole career, he took especial interest in the Canadian "Historical Society," furnishing it with an interesting sketch of the incidents of the war of 1812–1815 which came under his immediate notice, and giving such other information, as, from his position in the navy, he was possessed of.

Nor were the old veterans who had fought for the same cause as he had, nor the aged settlers with whom he had associated in his early years, overlooked or forgotten, now that he was in the decline of life.

On the formation of the association of the York Pioneers, he considered it not at all out of place for him to associate himself with them, though it was a purely secular society, and he took a very warm interest in their proceedings. The following extracts from papers furnished to the author, show the relation the Bishop held to the York Pioneers, and the estimation in which he was held by them:

Memo. of Dr. Richardson's connection with the York Pioneers.

Shortly after the organization of the York Pioneers (an association designed to perpetuate historical reminiscences of the early settlement of the town and county of York, and to bring together in social intercourse the surviving inhabitants of the locality), Dr. Richardson, who had for nearly fifty years been a resident in it, became a member. His advanced age, high position in the community, and, above all, his many estimable qualities, soon placed him in the President's chair, which he continued to fill at the unanimous desire of his associates, up to the time of his lamented death.

They will ever bear in affectionate remembrance the lively interest he at all times evinced for the success of the association, and the genial manner in which he presided at its meetings, whether for business or social enjoyment. With a memory well stored with facts and anecdotes of early times, he delighted in the opportunities these gatherings afforded him of relating them; while those who were privileged to listen to his interesting addresses at the annual festivals, will recall with pleasure the historic incidents and the wise and patriotic sentiments with which they abounded.

At a numerously attended meeting of the Pioneers, held shortly after his decease, the following minute was adopted, and ordered to be communicated to the family of their lamented friend, with the sincere expressions of sympathy under mutual loss :

" The Association of York Pioneers find it difficult to express adequately their deep sense of the loss which they have experienced in the death of their late venerated President, Rev. James Richardson, D.D. In common with the whole community, they mourn the removal from their midst of one who was truly eminent for his public and private virtues; distinguished by the manifestation throughout a long life, and in a singular variety of spheres of action, of sterling qualities, which will render his memory, as a Christian and as a man, ever dear to themselves, and of inestimable value to the country at large."

CHAPTER IX.

Increased activity after the death of Bishop Smith—Remarkable mental and physical vigor—Pains-taking as presiding officer—General Conference of 1874—Election and ordination of Bishop Carman—Last scene in Bishop Richardson's conferential life—Ill, and obliged to leave the Conference room as soon as he had placed his associate in the chair—Relief and satisfaction afforded him by the appointment of his colleague—Recovery and return to former activity—Last pulpit services—Last text—Incidents of homeward journey—Last illness—State of his mind—Death.

The years between 1865 and 1870 passed without being marked by any special event, the time being filled up by the ordinary routine duties of his office, with this exception, that as Bishop Smith grew more and more feeble with age, and, in consequence, became more incapacitated for carrying out that part of the work allotted to him, Bishop Richardson became correspondingly more active, being determined that no department of church work should suffer from the failing health of his honored colleague.

In March, 1870, the saintly Smith passed over the flood, and for nearly the whole of the remaining five years of Bishop Richardson's life, the entire weight of this responsible office rested upon him, then in his eightieth year. The amount of work accomplished by Bishop Richardson, during the four years, from 1870 to 1874, would have worn out the constitution of many younger men; but with additional labor and responsibility, came additional bodily strength. Indeed, for a time, he seemed almost to have renewed, if not his youth, at least the vigor of mature manhood. For two or three years previous to his death, it might have been said of him, as was said of the ancient leader and law-giver of the hosts of Israel, that "his eye was not dim;" and though it could not be averred that "his natural force was not abated," yet it might very truthfully have been said that few men of his years possessed his vigor.

During this period he frequently conducted his pulpit services without the aid of spectacles, and also the business of Conference. Nor did he make his dispensing with glasses an excuse for accomplishing less personal labor than before, in the Conference room. He kept a record of the business transacted in the Conferences, so that he might see that all the items were taken up in their proper order, and thus prevent irregularities. The Conferences latterly considered the task quite too laborious for him, and repeatedly offered him the assistance of a private secretary; but he persistently refused the proffered aid.

For a year or two past it became evident that his system was beginning to give way, although the Bishop himself did not seem to realize that this was the case. In labors he still continued abundant. It was simply astonishing the number of churches which he dedicated, and the other public meetings of importance over which he presided, in various parts of the Province, during the two years preceding his death.

He still presided over the Conferences, and other associations of which he was president, with remarkable ability, and his decisions upon points of ecclesiastical law were as clear, concise, and in as full accord with the constitution of the Church as they had ever been. In his pulpit exercises he was nearly as vigorous as in his earlier ministerial career.

We come now to his last discharge of the duties pertaining to his office, at the General Conference held at Napanee, August, 1874. Here the energies of his body and mind were taxed to the uttermost; yet he conducted the business of the Conference with patience and ability; and, until nearly the close of the lengthy session, without apparent fatigue.

Four years previously he had been desirous for the appointment and consecration of a suitable person as his associate in office, that he might be relieved of part of his labor; and now the desire for such an associate amounted to extreme solicitude. When, therefore, Rev. Dr. Carman was elected, the venerable patriarch appeared anxious for the moment to arrive when he might ordain his longed-for colleague, alas! so soon to become his successor. An evening session was appointed for the solemn service, and by the time the hour had arrived, the church was crowded to witness the impressive ceremony.

The proper arrangements having been made, Bishop Richardson entered the altar to proceed with the ordination. None then knew that he was about to exercise, for the last time, his duties as a Bishop. Venerable and noble in person, benign and dignified in appearance, his usually pale countenance crowned by his snowy locks, it is no wonder that he was the principal object of attraction on that eventful evening.

He stated to one of the brethren near him that he was very ill; scarcely able to proceed with the service; but that he felt the ordination of the Bishop elect must be proceeded with at once, as he was unable to conduct the remaining business of the Conference, and close it as he wished it to be done.

Having rested a little, and all being in readiness, Dr. Carman, as Bishop elect, and the brethren selected to take part in the exercises being assembled around the altar railing, the Bishop proceeeded with the Consecration Service, and ordained Albert Carman, D.D., to the office of Bishop in the Methodist Episcopal Church in Canada. After the conclusion of the ordination services, which all the circumstances contributed to render remarkably impressive, the aged Bishop appeared somewhat refreshed, and concluded his part of the exercises with an address to the Conference and congregation, on the scriptural polity of the Church, and the success the Lord of the harvest had vouchsafed to this branch of His Zion.

This was his last address to a Conference—his last conferential act.

Bishop Richardson, having placed Bishop Carman in the chair to finish up the business of the session, retired to obtain rest.

It is rather a strange coincidence that Bishop Richardson, having been so unusually hale for a man of his years, and having borne the work and worry of the Conference with so little apparent fatigue till the appointment of the new Bishop, should have been compelled by physical suffering to leave the Conference room as soon as he had placed his associate in the chair.

He evidently experienced the same feelings as Moses did when he exclaimed, " Let the Lord, the God of the spirits of all flesh set a man over the congregation which may go out before them, and which may go in before them, and which may lead them out and which may bring them in; that the congregation of the Lord be not as sheep which have no shepherd. And as Joshua was the man appointed to lead the people on to conquest in Canaan after Moses should be gathered to his fathers, so was Dr. Carman selected to lead the host of the Methodist Episcopal Church in Canada on to glorious spiritual conquests. "Moses laid his hands on Joshua, and the children of Israel hearkened unto him and did as the Lord commanded Moses;" and from the excellent spirit manifested by the ministers and people of our Church towards Bishop Carman since his appointment to the General Superintendency of the Church, it is fair to infer that the entire connexion is ready to exclaim, "All that thou commandest us, we will do, and whithersoever thou sendest us, we will go."

"According as we have hearkened unto Moses in all things, so will we hearken unto thee; only the Lord thy God be with thee as he was with Moses."

Reference has been made to Bishop Richardson's earnest wish for an associate in office. He was now very far advanced in years, and needed assistance in his arduous labors, and in addition, he fully realized the fact that it was not probable he would live to preside over another General Conference, and he was exceedingly anxious that the coming Bishop should be a man of marked and judicial ability, of undoubted piety, and whose attachment to the distinctive features of our Church polity was not only unquestioned, but unquestionable.

All these requisites he believed Dr. Carman possessed in an eminent degree, and he was therefore well pleased with the selection made by the Conference.

After the close of the General Conference, Bishop Richardson returned to his home at Cloverhill, Toronto, where he rested for some time, and, to appearance, regained his accustomed health. In October, he met with the Book Committee in Hamilton, presiding with his usual ability.

During the autumn and winter he was

actively at work, as earnestly as ever watching over every department of the Church, giving especial attention to the questions submitted by the General Conference for the action of the Quarterly Meeting Conferences. His articles on all Church matters published in *The Canada Christian Advocate*, were still very clear, and his views of constitutional questions forcibly presented and firmly maintained. And in these last judicial utterances he was careful to show his esteemed junior colleague all due respect. If we have been correctly informed, he never sent an official line to the press, after the General Conference at Napanee, without consulting Bishop Carman, and having his full concurrence thereto. Besides the official labor referred to above, he attended numerous dedications, anniversaries, and other public demonstrations, preaching and presiding with great acceptability. His appearance, and the manner in which he conducted his part of the dedicatory service at Strathroy, in the winter, will not soon be forgotten by those whose privilege it was to be present.

Bishop Richardson's last public services were held on the Ancaster Circuit. He had arranged with Rev. W. H. Shaw to preach the anniversary sermon at Salem Church, on this circuit, on Sabbath, 21st of February.

Whenever he could do so, he preferred travelling by his own conveyance rather than by rail, as he very much disliked inhaling the foul air with which the cars are generally charged, in consequence of a lack of proper ventilation; and as he had ascertained that a son of Mr. Shaw, who was then residing in Toronto, purposed going to Ancaster at the same time, he arranged for the young man to go with him and drive, the distance being about sixty miles; thus he thought he would avoid unnecessary exposure on the one hand, and the annoyance of the cars on the other; and, in addition, it would afford him an opportunity of visiting several old, tried friends, with whom he delighted to review the past, and anticipate a prosperous future for the Church.

The Bishop and his young companion left Cloverhill on the morning of the 19th of

February, and although the weather was cold, they journeyed on with tolerable comfort, and reached the residence of Mr. Peter Fisher, of Port Nelson, sometime in the afternoon of that day. Mr. Fisher and the Bishop had been old acquaintances of over forty years standing, and during all that time had maintained a warm personal friendship with each other. The evening was spent in the most social, agreeable, and profitable manner, talking over the past history of the Church, and of the country, with which both men had grown old. The Bishop's memory was very retentive, and he was particularly correct in giving dates, so that his conversation, interspersed as it was with incidents in relation to the early settlement of the country, was extremely interesting. Mr. and Mrs. Fisher had always highly appreciated the Bishop's visits to their house, and never were they more pleased and profited with one, than on this occasion.

On Saturday the travellers reached the Ancaster Parsonage, where every attention was paid to the Bishop's comfort by Brother and Sister Shaw, and their family. Salem church was distant from the parsonage a few miles, and the Bishop was driven over in the morning. He preached to a crowded house, with great freedom and power, from 1st Peter i: 3rd and 4th verses; and again in the evening, in the village of Ancaster, from Phil. i: 21, "For me to live is Christ, and to die is gain." How suitable a text for his last proclamation of the glorious Gospel of Christ. Speaking of the Bishop's preaching that day, Mr. Shaw says: "The friends remarked to me on the unction and power which accompanied his words." On Monday evening he attended the anniversary tea-meeting in the Salem church, where he met several of the preachers, with whom he conversed freely in relation to various matters concerning the general interests of the Church; and also delivered his excellent lecture on "The early settlement of Canada." This was his last public appearance; his work was almost done.

On Tuesday, he and young Mr. Shaw set out on their return to Toronto, the Bishop to all appearances in his usual health. They dined and rested for the time at Mr. Peter Fisher's, and that afternoon proceeded to Palermo, where they remained over night, stopping with Dr. Buck. The evening at Dr. Buck's was spent in a manner similar to the one spent at Mr. Fisher's the week previous. After family worship the Bishop retired, still apparently well, and as was his custom, rose early next morning. He conducted the family worship that morning, commenting freely on the lesson read, and engaged in prayer with great freedom. That morning, while seated at the breakfast table, he remarked to the Dr. and his wife, that he had had a singular dream the night before. He dreamed, he said, that his mother, who had been dead over sixty years, came to him, and appeared very pleasant, and as natural as when he had seen her last in his youth. He was but eighteen when she died, and he had not dreamt of her before for many years. The conversation turned on the singularity of dreams, sometimes, and the matter dropped without further explanation. Shortly after breakfast, the journey towards home was resumed, but they had travelled only a short distance when he remarked to Shaw, "Hector, I feel so strangely. I never felt so before. My sight is so dim." The young man suggested that it might be the reflection of the sun upon the snow, but the Bishop insisted that that could not be the cause of the dizziness he experienced, and of the strange sensations affecting his whole system. They drove as rapidly as possible to the house of a brother Stafford, on Dundas St. He was urged to lie down, but refused to do so, resting, however, in an easy chair. At dinner he ate very sparingly, and afterwards still continued to complain of dizziness in his head, and feeling so strangely. Being anxious to reach home they left Mr. Stafford's shortly after dinner, he being still troubled with the dizziness and occasional dimness of sight. During the drive home he conversed with his young friend, at intervals, in his usual kind and instructive manner, giving him a short synopsis of the history of the Mormons, and also conversing at some length on the subject of future punishment, and on some of the striking features of Romanism. They reached home about four o'clock P.M., and the Bishop at once sought rest. He rested pretty well through the night, and met his young friend at breakfast next morning; and on bidding him good bye, promised to revisit Ancaster Circuit on the 9th of March—the very day on which he died. Becoming worse, he sent for his son, Dr. J. H. Richardson, who entertained but slight hopes of his recovery from the moment he saw him. Everything was done to relieve him, that medical skill could devise, or that affection could suggest, but he continued to sink away.

During his illness, which lasted from the 24th of February, till the 9th of March, the Bishop was visited from time to time, as prudence permitted, by a large number of the ministers of his own church, and also by those of other denominations in Toronto and vicinity. Rev. Mr. Shaw visited him on the day he was to have been with him in Ancaster, and remarks that the Bishop conversed with him concerning his future home, calmly, collectedly, and clearly. The conversation turned on his sermon delivered a short time since when he remarked, "all is well," then raising his arm and looking upwards, he uttered the following lines :

> "Rock of Ages cleft for me,
> Let me hide myself in Thee."

Even in those dying moments his thoughts were engaged on matters pertaining to the interests of the church. In the conversation with Mr. Shaw, from which the foregoing has been extracted, he inquired as to who was likely to succeed Bishop Carman in the College, &c. After Mr. Shaw had engaged in prayer with him, he bade him an affectionate farewell, sending also a kind farewell to Mrs. Shaw and the children. He died not long after Mr. Shaw left.

To another of the preachers who visited him, he said, "I have no ecstasy, but I know in whom I have believed." To yet another he remarked, "My work is done, I have nothing to do now but to die."

The character of his disease did not admit of his conversing long at a time, and therefore his sentences were short, but always forcible. His reason was clear, and with strong confidence in God, he calmly entered into his rest. The telegraph announced his death, not only to his immediate acquaintances, but throughout the Dominion, and next morning the daily papers communicated the fact to the thousands of his friends in the Provinces.

So soon as it was known in the city that the venerable Richardson was no more, the National flag on the Custom House was lowered to half mast, as were those on other public buildings, and on some of the vessels in the harbor.

CHAPTER X.

The funeral—By whom attended—The funeral sermon—Memorial services held throughout our work—A painful void felt at the Annual Conferences—Conference memorial services—Lines suggested by the sad bereavement.

On the 12th of March, 1875, the sorrowing friends met to pay their last tribute of respect to him who had been so highly honored, and so much beloved during his life. The funeral was largely attended by the Ministers of his own Church and by some of other churches from various parts of Canada, and by those of the various Protestant denominations in Toronto, as well as by very many leading citizens.

Some idea of the high esteem which was entertained for this venerable man of God may be gathered from the notice of the funeral which appeared in the *Globe* of March 13th, 1875, and which we insert after making a few verbal corrections. The account given was as nearly correct as such accounts generally are; the reporter could not be expected to do more than set down the names of a few of the more prominent representative men who were present, but hundreds of worthy men were in attendance who were unknown to these caterers for the reading public. It has been stated that a larger number of ministers were present than ever before attended any funeral in Toronto.

The report is as follows:

"Yesterday afternoon the funeral of the late Rev. James Richardson, D.D., Bishop of the Methodist Episcopal Church, took place from his late residence at Clover Hill, the remains of deceased being interred in the vault at the Necropolis."

The friends and mourners met at the residence of the deceased shortly before three o'clock, at which hour an impressive service was held by Bishop Carman, of the Methodist Episcopal Church in Canada, assisted by Revs. M. Benson and G. Abbs.

"The coffin which was of polished walnut with heavy silver mountings, bore the following inscription:—"James Richardson, born January 29th, 1791, died March 9th, 1875.

"The funeral procession, which was a very lengthened one, started from the house of mourning about half-past three o'clock. First came the members of the York Pioneers' Society, of which deceased was President, followed by Col. R. L. Denison, Col. R. B. Denison, Rev. Dr. Scadding, Archdeacon Fuller, Messrs. Philip Armstrong, A. Hamilton, Dr. Geo. Crawford, E. Edmunds, John Bell, Q.C., Rev. J. Carroll, J. McMullen, R. James, R. Leore, J. T. Smith, James Gedd, J. Stitt, R. H. Oates, W. B. Phipps, J. Bostwick, D. Sampson. A. Heron, J. Bugg, J. White, D. O. Brooke, Dr. H. Wright, Dr. R. Hornby, A. T. McCord, S. Rogers, R. L. Smith, G. H. Holland, W. J. Coate, T. Burgess, W. Barnhard, J. Farrell, T. Meredith, R. Dodds, F. Milligan, Rev. S. Givins, S. Bowman, J. Jacques, J. W. Drummond, J. Paul, Dr. Jas. Small, J. Playter, W. Gooderham, J. G. Worts, B. Bull, W. J. Storm, W. Edwards."

"Immediately preceding the hearse were Bishop Carman, Thomas Webster, D.D., Revs. M. Benson, G. Abbs, M. A. Wright, J. McLean, S. S. Stone, Rev. Dr. Ryerson, Dean Grassett, Revs. Wm. Reid, W. H. Shaw, Saltern Givins, T. Baker, Rev. Mr. Baldwin, and Mr. A. T. McCord. Next came the hearse, followed by the ministers of the Methodist Episcopal Church— Revs. F. M. Finn, Percy ; T. Agnew, Brampton ; J. Lynch, Rockwood ; R. E. Lund, Cobourg ; E. J. Pelley, Dundas ; J. Sampson, Brighton ; J. Miller, Colborne ; J. Curts, Weston ; J. S. Williamson,

Hamilton; E. Londesberry, Strathroy; Revs. Dr. Wild, Brooklyn, New York; R. Denick, Palermo; J. Gilray, Toronto; W. S. Brown, Lyndon; R. Large, Whitterdale; A. Beamer, Ingersoll. The chief mourners were Dr. Jas. H. Richardson, deceased's son; Dr. Robert D. Richardson, deceased's grandson; Master W. Roaf, and Master J. Roaf, deceased's grandchildren; Mr. Henry Denis, of Weston. Next came the representatives of the Upper Canada Bible and Tract Societies, Messrs. J. K. McDonald, J. A. R. Dickson, Robt. Baldwin, Dr. J. G. Hodgins, and the representatives of Toronto Temperance Reformation Society, which deceased was originator of, and for several years its President. Many friends also followed in the procession, among others Canon Baldwin, Revs. J. Potts, W. H. Poole, S. Rose, S. N. Jackson, F. H. Marling, etc. The procession proceeded by way of Yonge Street, Carlton Street, and Winchester Street, to the Necropolis, where the burial service was performed by Bishop Carman, after which the coffin was placed in the receiving vault."

The funeral sermon was preached by Bishop Carman, in the Metropolitan Methodist church, Toronto, on Sunday morning, March 21st, the use of the church having been kindly offered to the Bishop by the Rev. Mr. Potts, the pastor of the congregation worshiping in that beautiful Temple of the Lord.

The congregation was large, " among whom were most of the members of the York Pioneers' Society." Bishop Carman took for his text 1st Corinthians, xv. 55: "O death, where is thy sting? O grave, where is thy victory?" We can only give a few short extracts from this eloquent discourse:

"The text," said the speaker, "is one of the Apostle Paul's magnificent exultations. It is the leap of a robust spirit; the bound of a noble soul. It is the outburst of a suppressed emotion; the explosion of a pent up fire. It is the mounting of the eagle into the tracts of the air; the spring of the steed for the freedom of the plains. It is not merely the quick delight of sense, or the sudden flame of passion. It is not the mere gloating of the appetite, or the fondness of the desire. It is not the mere pleasure of sentiment; or the flash of thought. It is not merely the happy radiance of reason, or the joyous triumph of argument. It is all that is good, and pure, and sound, and solid in all these; but it is also far more than all these. It has all that sense, and emotion, and sentiment, and reason, and argument can give; but it has something rapturous and sublime that they cannot all, to-

gether, give. It is the majestic flight of faith in God; the outreaching of the immortal mind to grasp its glorious destiny. From the firm foundation, the immovable rock of fact, and testimony, and reason, and argument; from the character and government, and promises of Jehovah, the soul mounts vigorously upward, and soars amid the splendours of the imperial sun. This is the leap of faith; its grand excursion in the light ineffable. Surely the bird of the mountain, plunging into the aerial ocean from his rocky height, and with swift wing cleaving the sky, has wider and nobler range than the reptile crawling about the mountain's base, or the sure-footed beast climbing its rugged sides. The former has all the possessions of the latter, but also has much more. To the one no less than to the other, the bald granite, the gorge, the precipice and the slopes are realities, indispensable realities. To the one no less than to the other is the mountain the life. But the grander flight finds even grander realities in the broader, purer fields of light and air. So faith, despising not, neglecting not, forsaking not fact and reason, mounts upward from fact and reason to the eternal verities of the moral Government of God, and the moral and immortal nature of man. * * * * * * *
There are elevations of trust in God; lofty joys of communion with Him, and sublime realizations of

His power that unaided reason knows nothing of. And this was the rapture of Paul; not without reason, but leaping forth from it with an alacrity and an energy mightily above it. These exultations, these bursting joys of the combined glories of reason, and sentiment, and faith were characteristic of the great preacher to the Gentile world. He clearly states the fact; he urges the argument; he gazes upon the transcendant glory; he believes with all his heart in the immeasureable goodness and the irresistible power of the God of his love, till the rising tide of his emotion breaks over every barrier of his attempted restraint, fills every capacity of his soul, and brightens and freshens every faculty of his being. The argument is complete; the demonstration is secure; the grandeur is manifest; and then the joy abounds. The irrepressible rapture, in the full-flood tide of glory, rolls over the soul. This is the habit of his mind, the ecstacy of the abundant revelation. So it is in that inimitable argument for justification by faith without the deeds of the law. He has proved that all men are alike under sin; that in man's moral nature there is no help; that the law frowns only to condemn. 'O, wretched man that I am, who shall deliver me from the body of this death?' 'I thank God, through Jesus Christ our Lord. There is therefore now no condemnation to them that are in Christ Jesus, who walk not after the flesh, but after the spirit.' 'Heirs of God and joint heirs with Christ.' Having shown the nature of the spiritual life, the regeneration and sanctification of the human soul through the operation of the Holy Ghost; having declared the witness of the Spirit of God to our adoption, and the loving attachment of the sons of God to their Father in heaven he breaks forth: 'Who shall separate us from the love of God? Shall tribulation, or distress, or persecution, or famine, or nakedness, or peril, or sword? Nay, in all these things we are more than conquerors through Him that loved us. For I am persuaded that neither death, nor life, nor angels, nor principalities, nor powers, nor things present, nor things to come, nor height, nor depth, nor any other creature shall be able to separate us from the love of God which is in Christ Jesus our Lord.' As also Wesley: 'Now I have found the ground wherein,' &c. Having demonstrated that the gifts and callings of God are without repentance; that the election of his people, whether Jew or Gentile, proceeded upon their character of repentance, faith, and obedience; having descended with his people through the awful calamity and sorrow of their rejection of God on account of their sins, and having risen again to the grand conception of the comprehensive plan of the Eternal Father to embrace all nations of men in the great salvation by faith in Jesus Christ, he rapturously exclaims: 'O, the depth of the riches both of the wisdom and knowledge of God! How unsearchable are His judgments, and His ways past finding out. For who hath known the mind of the Lord? or who hath been His counsellor? or who hath first given to Him, and it shall be recompensed unto him again. For of Him, and through Him, and to Him, are all things; to whom be glory for ever! Amen!'"

* * * * * * * * *

After pointing out at considerable length the blessedness of the Gospel, which enables the believer to triumph over death and the grave, through the blessed atonement; and after giving a historical account of the life and labors, patriotic and ministerial, of his late colleague, Bishop Carman concluded a long and able sermon with the words following:

"And now what shall we say in summing up the character of this great and good man? In every sphere of life into which he came, he filled its full orb with his energy and his power. In the domestic circle, in society, in the nation and in the church, he was the complete man. In private and in public virtues he was a model for the people. He was firm without being dogmatic; he was mild without being easy and indifferent. He loved his home without neglecting his country. He served his country without slighting his home. In counsel, the sage; in action, the hero; in manner, the gentleman; in conversation, the historian and the philosopher; how shall we supply his place, or when shall we look upon his like again? He leaves to his family, his church, his country, the heritage of a spotless character. They need not mourn: but may better arise and emulate his virtues. Do you seek an ardent patriotism? You find it in James Richardson. Do you seek an untarnished honour, and unblemished reputation? You find them in James Richardson. Do you seek a sincere philanthropy? You find it in James Richardson. Would you have a keen sense of duty, an exalted appreciation of justice, a firm adherence to truth, and a sober and unaffected, a deep and all-pervading, piety? You will find them in James Richardson. As a soldier, he was faithful and brave. As a man of business, he was honourable and obliging. As a preacher, he was zealous and effective. As a bishop, and an administrator of discipline, he was candid, careful and correct. In plain exposition of the blessed doctrines of the Bible he had no superior; in knowledge of church discipline and ecclesiastical policy and usage, perhaps not an equal in the country.

His shining abilities, his splendid equilibrium of faculties, would have made him a power in Parliament, or an ornament to the Bench. But he counted all these but loss, that he might win Christ. He dedicated all to God. He laid all at the foot of the cross. Thereby he was enabled to be abundantly useful in his generation, and has gone to a rich reward."

It was deemed but fitting to have memorial services held throughout the connexion, as there were thousands, who, while desirous of honoring his memory, were yet unable to attend the funeral services. Therefore Bishop Carman, with the concurrence of several of his brethren present on that occasion, decided to recommend that such services be held throughout the connexion, as far as practicable, on Sunday, March 28th.

The proposition was well received, and on that day our ministers, generally, called the attention of their people to the consideration of the high character, patriotic career, public usefulness, blameless life, and abundant Christian efforts of this good man, and able minister of the Lord Jesus Christ.

It will not be possible, in the compass of

this work, to give even an outline of these religious services. They were all, necessarily, very similar in character, the congregations varying in numbers according to different localities. It is hoped that these memorial services of this "prince in our Israel" have been the means of leading many souls to Christ.

The meetings of the Annual Conferences were, at their commencement, seasons of deep sorrow and of some anxiety. The chair so long occupied by the venerable Bishop was vacant; and, while the preachers were glad to know that, in his learned and affable successor, they possessed a presiding officer in every way fitted to fill that chair, they could not but grieve that they would see no more on earth the face of that friend who had been as a spiritual father to so many of them, but who would now never more guide them by his mature counsels.

The Conference memorial services were attended with excellent effects, both upon the preachers themselves and upon the congregations in attendance.

The " workmen die, but the work goes on."
" The Lord God Omnipotent reigneth."

The author has pleasure in presenting to the many admiring friends of our late beloved Bishop, the following appreciative lines, composed by Mrs. ISABELLA BAILEY WEBSTER WALLACE.

LINES SUGGESTED BY THE DEATH AND BURIAL OF THE LATE BISHOP RICHARDSON.

No martial pomp, no muffled drum, no tattered colours trailing low,
No solemn dirge, no booming gun, hints of the ancient well-fought foe
Whom he had met with dauntless front, while with a sailor's honest pride
He steered his barque, 'mid smoke and flame, o'er blue Ontario's heaving tide.
No fear had he of shot or shell, or of the yawning, hungry wave;
His only thought, from foreign arms, his much loved native land to save.
Nor repined he at the soldier's fate, although so early maimed for life,
But with returning vigor, came again to join the fearful strife.
No veteran* of that sturdy band, who then obeyed his hearty call,
Is mingling with the saddened throng, who follow now his funeral pall.
The brave, the true, who may survive, have vanished from our sight and ken,
And all the victories which they won, were nullified by weaker men.
But comrades in a holier war, true soldiers of a mightier King,
Are here from well contested fields, and faithful, loving hearts they bring.
They've come, to gaze with lingering look, on that dear face they loved so well;
But ah! they miss the kindling eye, the smile where welcome used to dwell.
They miss that voice, so mild, so deep, which charmed them in their boyhood's days,

* One of Mr. Richardson's comrades on the *St. Lawrence* was present at his funeral, as one of the pall-bearers, but he was not with him at Oswego.

Which oft had sounded in their ears, in admonition or in praise.
Their sorrow, not like transient cloud, whose shadow for an instant lies,
Blackening the verdant vales of June, then in a moment onward flies.
'Tis such as weighs the loftiest down, when they behold their noble dead,
And realize that life is o'er, that all that was *their friend* has fled.
In that cold form, serenely calm, they still his lineaments may trace,
But now loved tones unheeded fall, no answering smile illumes the face.
The soul, that glorious spark divine, which was, *and is* the real man,
Has cast aside this garb of clay, which lies so mute, so pale, so wan.
Now from their very sorrow, springs a joy which is the Christian's own;
The soldier who had fought so well, is placed before his Sovereign's throne.
No more the weary, toilsome march; no more the conflict with the waves;
No more to feel the serpent's fangs, no more to weep o'er new-made graves.
But in the presence of his Lord, for evermore he sits him down,
And he who bore the cross so long, now wears the victor's glorious crown.
Radiant with stars, which far surpass the brightness of the rising day,
They speak of souls, who, by his words, were led to own Jehovah's sway.
This thought, of his supreme delight, has soothing power amid their grief;
Oh! may his spotless mantle, falling, rest upon their youthful chief.
Oh! may the Church, through all the land, thrill with a purer, warmer flame;
Still, in her earnest war with ill, keep ever bright her honored name.
And those few silvery-headed men, who watched with him our country's rise,
May they, too, find a lasting home, with him, beyond the arching skies.

Then those dear sorrowing ones, whose love is not the growth of years,
But was implanted in their hearts, ere they had known life's cares or fears;
May they, by following close *his* steps, who guided their's through youth's wild maze,
Be brought to share his glorious rest, and join with him in heavenly lays.
Oh! may his children's children seek, whate'ver in life may them betide,
The love of God, their father's King. May He with them for aye abide.

ZELL'S POPULAR ENCYCLOPEDIA

AND

UNIVERSAL DICTIONARY

New and Revised Edition, with 18 Coloured Maps.

THIS work furnishes a complete description of every subject connected with History, Biography, Geography, Science, Art, Language, Natural History, Botany, Mineralogy, Medicine, Law, Mechanics, Architecture, Manufacturing, Agriculture, Bible History, Church History, Religions, &c.

It is, in fact, equal to a complete library of works on all subjects.

Printed in ordinary type and page, it would make **Twenty Volumes**, worth not less than $5 each, or $100 for the entire work.

It contains nearly 150,000 articles, all prepared with great care, by the most able authors, each specially qualified for his particular part.

An article in the *National Quarterly*, edited by Ed. I. Sears, LL.D., gives the views of that able and scholarly reviewer and critic upon this work.

He begins with remarking that he had received not less than fifty letters within the year, asking his opinion of Zell's Popular Encyclopedia.

From a prejudice against the word "**popular**," as too often used in this country, the Doctor confesses that, **before examining** it, his faith in the new Encyclopedia was very slight. After a careful examination, he speaks of it, with unqualified commendation, as follows:

"'Blessed,' he says, quoting Swift, 'are they that expect nothing, for they shall not be disappointed.' If we are not blessed, we are at least agreeably surprised. The prefix **popular**, as generally used in this country, is not appropriate in this **present** instance, but in the sense of **instructive** and useful to **all classes** of the **people** who have any taste for the acquisition of knowlgdge, or any desire for extending the sphere of their intelligence; and, in this sense, we know no similar work to which it may be more justly applied. In other words, the new Encyclopedia is not the crude, shallow, slip-shod, self-contradictory sort of performance which so many of our authors and compilers seem to regard as only suitable for the people, and the only kind that ought to be called **popular**. It is a work which, while it must prove attractive, as well as useful, to those who have received only the most elementary education, cannot fail to recommend

ZELL'S POPULAR ENCYCLOPEDIA.

itself, also, to the most highly educated, even to possessors of good libraries, for the large amount of information, in general, well digested and accurate, which it embraces on multiform subjects, including the whole circle of the Arts and Sciences. Many articles are quite long and elaborate. The majority owe their value to the circumstance that in their condensed form they rarely omit any important particular, and scarcely ever any newly-discovered fact. Thus the literary and scientific labourer is often enabled to **obtain at a glance** information requiring extensive research elsewhere, and which is not to **be found at all** in **other** Encyclopedias. It affords us pleasure to bear testimony to the peculiar merits of this work. The departments which please us most are the Historical, Geographical, Archæological, and Scientific. In the department of Science, we have sufficient of what is not found in **any** similar work, being the result of recent research and discoveries, to recommend the work. The Lexicographical department **alone** is of **great** value; it is indeed such that none having it will have any need to pay the high price demanded at the present day for a copy of Webster's Dictionary. The numerous and generally accurate illustrations of Zell's Popular Encyclopedia considerably enchance the interest and attractiveness."

The following notices are from the *Globe* and *Mail:*

"This work, which will be exceedingly useful as a book of reference, is published in numbers, sixty-four of which are to complete the whole. It is edited by L. Colange, L.L.D., is handsomely printed, and contains 18 beautiful maps, besides numerous illustrative Engravings. Whilst aiming at scientific accuracy, it is at the same time intended to be popular, the articles being written in plain language. . . . In order to show the value of the work to every one, we will mention that it is a complete dictionary of language; it contains every word, with its etymology and definition, that is to be found in other large dictionaries. It is also a complete gazeteer."

"The plan of this work is wonderfully comprehensive, embracing as it does a dictionary of language, a biographical and a medical dictionary, a history of the world, a complete natural history, a complete work on botany, also on Mechanics, and a Church history. In short, there is no subject to which reference is not made. All who want a book to which they can turn in a moment for anything in the world they want to know about, will find ZELL'S ENCYCLOPEDIA just what they require."

This work is published in 2, 3, 4 and 5 volume editions, varying in price from $37 50 to $75 per set; and in 64 parts at fifty cents each.

Full particulars, (specimen part with a map, post-paid for twenty-five cents) will be sent on application. Sold only by subscription.

J. B. MAGURN,
PUBLISHERS' GENERAL AGENT,
36 King Street East, Toronto.

P. O. Box 743.

PRAYER

AND ITS

REMARKABLE ANSWERS.

A Statement of Facts in the Light of Reason and Revelation.

BY REV. WM. W. PATTON, D.D.

This work covers ground occupied by no other book. Its theme is one of **absorbing interest** to the Christian, and it is believed that a perusal of its pages will not fail to deeply interest **all classes of people**. It will confound, if not convince, the sceptic, strengthen the faith of Believers, and awaken to earnest thought the Impenitent.

The author has given, in **popular form**, both the facts and the philosophy of the subject. It is written for the **people**, yet it assumes that they are neither children nor fools, but desire *an intelligent discussion of a fundamental question*. The heads of the chapters, herewith, will serve to show how thoroughly the subject has been handled by the author.

It will be observed that about **one-third** of the book is devoted to the **nature, characteristics, methods and conditions of Prayer**, and the remaining **two-thirds** to **Striking Cases of Answers to Prayer**, for all variety of objects. The cases quoted are largely original, and have been furnished the author from **trustworthy sources**, and in most instances the sources are given. These have been culled from a much larger number that were supplied to the author expressly for this work, but which had to be omitted for want of space. They are arranged carefully in distinct Chapters, to illustrate the success of prayer for *different objects*, and are accompanied by explanatory and critical remarks. It is a book which every Pastor will welcome, as helpful to the progress of piety in his church, and which will encourage the Christian to ask and expect greater blessings for himself and for others.

PRAYER AND ITS REMARKABLE ANSWERS.

CONTENTS.

Chapter I. Prayer characteristic of Piety.—II. What true Prayer is.—III. Why Prayer prevails.—IV. The method of the answer.—V. Conditions of success in Prayer.—VI. The Prayer of Faith.—VII. Sceptical assaults on Prayer.—VIII. Bible-answers to Prayer—Old Testament.—IX. Bible-answers to Prayer—New Testament.—X. Prayer for the supply of temporal wants (commenced).—XI. Prayer for the supply of temporal wants (concluded).—XII. Prayer for physical healing (commenced).—XIII. Prayer for physical healing (concluded).—XIV. Prayer for sanctifying grace.—XV. Prayer to overcome physical habit.—XVI. Prayer for individual conversions.—XVII. Parental Prayers.—XVIII. Prayer for ministers, churches and revivals.—XIX. Prayer for charitable institutions.—XX. Review of facts in conclusion. 403 pages.

The Rev. JOHN POTTS gives the following opinion of this book.

"I have somewhat carefully examined Dr. Patton's book entitled 'Prayer and its Remarkable Answers.' The subject is one of undying interest to finite beings, and its treatment by the author is intelligent, interesting and practical. The perusal of these pages must give greatly enlarged views of the nature, obligation and privilege of Prayer.

"Those who habitually 'bow before the God and Father of our Lord Jesus Christ' will feel especially encouraged to expect large blessings, as they learn of the remarkable answers recorded on the pages of this book.

"JOHN POTTS.

"METROPOLITAN CHURCH PARSONAGE,
"TORONTO, *February*, 1876."

English cloth, black and gold, $1.50; gilt edges, $2.00.

J. B. MAGURN,
PUBLISHER,
36 King Street East, Toronto.

www.ingramcontent.com/pod-product-compliance
Lightning Source LLC
Chambersburg PA
CBHW021344230426
43666CB00006B/406